The
Elements
of Copywriting

THE ESSENTIAL GUIDE TO
CREATING COPY THAT GETS
THE RESULTS YOU WANT

Also by Gary Blake and Robert W. Bly
The Elements of Business Writing
The Elements of Technical Writing

The
Elements
of
Copywriting

THE ESSENTIAL GUIDE TO
CREATING COPY THAT GETS
THE RESULTS YOU WANT

Gary Blake and Robert W. Bly

Longman

New York   San Francisco   Boston
London   Toronto   Sydney   Tokyo   Singapore   Madrid
Mexico City   Munich   Paris   Cape Town   Hong Kong   Montreal

ADDISON WESLEY LONGMAN
1185 Avenue of the Americas
New York, NY 10036

Library of Congress Cataloging-in-Publication Data

Bly, Robert W.

The elements of copywriting : the essential guide to creating copy that gets
the results you want / by Robert W. Bly and Gary Blake.

p.   cm.

Includes index.

ISBN 0-02-862630-3

1. Advertising copy. 2. Journalism—Authorship. I. Blake, Gary.
II. Title.
HF5825.B553   1997
659.13'2—dc21
97-2717
CIP

10 9 8 7

Printed in the United States of America

Contents

Acknowledgments

We'd like to thank our many copywriting clients, colleagues, students, and teachers. Mastering the art of copywriting is a lifelong process, and you have helped make the process fun and rewarding.

Introduction

Every day, hundreds of thousands of businesspeople—everyone from professional copywriters and publicists to entrepreneurs, middle managers, and presidents—write copy intended to sell, persuade, or educate customers about a product or service. These copywriting tasks include preparing ads, press releases, brochures, product descriptions, annual reports, speeches, sales letters, direct mail, telemarketing scripts, slide presentations, circulars, and Web sites.

The Elements of Copywriting aims to provide a style guide that speaks to the special tasks, formats, and terminology of copywriters and other promotional writers whose words define and sell our nation's goods and services.

Copywriting is a broad term. The words on a menu are *copy*. So are the words in an ad, product description, press release, annual report, announcement, invitation, package insert, sales letter, Web page, broadcast fax, CD-ROM presentation, and food label. Wherever there's a product or service, there's probably someone writing copy for it.

Today, poorly written, ineffective ads, press releases, catalogs, and brochures are the norm rather than the exception. Top professionals complain that recent college graduates are ill-equipped to write the type of succinct prose necessary to awaken an interest in ideas, organizations, products, and services. Many of today's copywriters have no guidelines for what constitutes good style.

Advertising copywriting has always made its own rules. While most business writers are taught to avoid redundancy, some of the best ad copy skillfully employs redundancy or the overuse of superlatives. While most of us are trained to avoid starting sentences with conjunctions, copywriters are urged to use conjunctions to improve flow and pace. While most business writers shun one-sentence paragraphs, copywriters use them frequently.

This book lays out the rules and reasons for how copywriters use language to awaken interest in—and generate sales of—products and services. It's written to appeal to two categories of readers.

The first category is the professional writer whose job it is to write copy. This category includes ad agency copywriters, advertising managers, sales promotion writers, technical writers, publicists, freelance writers, and marketing communications managers.

The second category is the businessperson who is not a full-time writer but is called upon to write or review copy for his or her company's products or services. This category includes marketing managers, brand managers, product managers, engineers, technicians, owners, presidents, entrepreneurs, senior executives, and secretaries.

With rampant downsizing and reduced budgets, nonwriters are increasingly being asked to write documents that once would have been assigned to staff or freelance professionals. Many of these nonwriters need guidance in this task. *The Elements of Copywriting* provides this guidance.

Part I of the book discusses the principles of effective copywriting. Part II gives rules and tips for specific copywriting tasks, such as newspaper ads, direct-mail packages, brochures, catalogs, press releases, audiovisual presentations, and Internet promotions.

Each chapter is divided into a series of short, numbered, easy-to-follow rules. The rules are succinct guidelines or principles and are illustrated with examples. We hope they help you create copy that gives you the results you desire.

The
Elements
of Copywriting

THE ESSENTIAL GUIDE TO
CREATING COPY THAT GETS
THE RESULTS YOU WANT

COPYWRITING PRINCIPLES

CHAPTER ONE

The Fundamentals of Persuasive Writing

W hat are the characteristics that make copy effective? Why does one ad make a lasting impression and sell a lot of merchandise, while another falls flat and doesn't generate enough revenue to pay its own cost?

Virtually all persuasive copy contains the eight elements described in this chapter. The successful ad does the following:

1. Gets attention

2. Focuses on the customer

3. Stresses benefits

4. Differentiates your product from the competition

5. Proves its case

6. Establishes credibility

7. Builds value

8. Closes with a call to action

Not all ads have all eight characteristics in equal proportions. Depending on the product, some of these elements will be dominant in your ad; others subordinate. But all eight elements must be present to some degree or the ad probably won't work.

Let's take telephone service as an example. Companies such as AT&T, MCI, and Sprint have well-established reputations and demonstrable records of success. Therefore, they will be strong in elements 5 and 6 (proving their case and establishing their credibility).

A new telephone service provider, on the other hand, does not have a track record or reputation; therefore, these two elements will not be the dominant themes in the copy. Instead, the strongest element might be 3 (benefits the service offers customers) or perhaps 4 (differentiation in service resulting from superior technology).

Let's take a look at these eight elements in detail and how they can be used to create effective advertising.

Element 1. Gain attention.

If an ad fails to gain attention, it fails totally because the prospects won't read any of your copy. And if the prospects don't read your copy, they won't receive the persuasive message you've so carefully crafted.

There are numerous ways to gain attention. Sex certainly is one of them. Look at the number of products—cars, clothes, cosmetics, soft drinks, chewing gum, sports equipment—that feature attractive bodies in their ads and commercials. It may be sexist or base, but it works.

Similarly, you can use visuals to get prospects to pay attention. Parents (and almost everyone else) are attracted to pictures of babies and young children. Puppies and kittens also strike a chord in our hearts. Appealing visuals can get your ad noticed.

Since so much advertising is vague and general, being specific in your copy sets it apart from other ads and creates interest. A letter promoting collection services to dental practices begins as follows:

> How we collected over <u>$20 million</u>
> in unpaid bills over the past two years
> for thousands of dentists nationwide
>
> Dear Dentist:
>
> It's true.
>
> In the past two years alone, IC Systems has collected more than <u>$20 million</u> in outstanding debt for dental practices nationwide.
>
> That's $20 million these dentists might not have recovered if they had not hired IC Systems to collect their past-due bills for them.

What gets your attention is the specific figure of $20 million dollars. Every collection agency promises to collect money. But saying that you have gotten $20 million in results is specific, credible, and memorable.

Featuring an offer that is free, low in price, or unusually attractive is also an effective attention-getter. A full-page newspaper ad from Guaranteed Term Life Insurance announces, "Now $1 a week buys Guaranteed Term Life Insurance for New Yorkers over 50." Not only does the $1 offer draw you in, but the headline also gains attention by targeting a specific group of buyers (New Yorkers over 50).

You know that in public speaking you can get attention by shouting or talking loudly. This direct approach can work in copy as well, especially in retail advertising. An ad for Lord & Taylor department store proclaims in large, bold type:

STARTS TODAY...ADDITIONAL 40% OFF WINTER FASHIONS

Not clever or fancy, but of interest to shoppers looking to save money.

Another method of engaging the prospect's attention is to ask a provocative question. *Bits & Pieces,* a management magazine, begins its subscription mailing with this headline: "What do Japanese managers have that American managers sometimes lack?" Don't you want to at least read the next sentence to find the answer?

A mailing for a book club has this headline on the outer envelope:

Why is the McGraw-Hill Chemical Engineers' Book Club giving away—practically for FREE—this special 50th Anniversary Edition of *Perry's Chemical Engineers' Handbook?*

To chemical engineers who know that the handbook costs about $125 per copy, the fact that someone would give it away is indeed a curiosity—and being curious people, engineers want the answer.

Injecting news into copy, or announcing something that is new or improved, is also a proven technique for getting attention. A self-mailer offering subscriptions to the newsletter *Dr. Atkins's Health Revelations* has this headline on the front cover:

Here Are Astonishing Nutritional Therapies and Alternative Treatments You'll *Never* Hear about from the Medical Establishment, the FDA, Drug Companies, or Even Your Doctor....

> Three decades of medical research breakthroughs from the
> Atkins Center for Complementary Medicine…revealed at last!

The traditional Madison Avenue approach to copy— subtle word-play and cleverness—often fails to get attention because many people reading the ad don't get it, or they do get it but don't think it's that funny, or they think it's funny but it doesn't compel them to buy the product. A newspaper ad for a New Jersey hospital, promoting its facilities for treating kidney stones without surgery (ultrasonic sound waves are used to painlessly break up and dissolve stones), carried this headline:

> The End of the Stone Age

Clever? Yes. But as former kidney stone patients, we can tell you that having kidney stones is not a fun, playful subject, and this headline misses the mark. The kidney stone sufferer wants to know he can go to the local hospital, get fast treatment, avoid an operation and a hospital stay, have the procedure be painless, and get rid of the kidney stones that are causing discomfort. Therefore, the headline

> Get Rid of Painful Kidney Stones—Without Surgery!

while less clever, is more direct, and works better with this topic and this audience.

Element 2. Focus on the customer.

When writing copy, start with the prospect, not with the product. Your prospects are interested primarily in themselves—their goals, their problems, their needs, their hopes, their fears, and their dreams. Your product or service is secondary to the potential of your product or service to address one of your prospects' wants or needs, or to solve one of their problems.

Effective copy speaks directly to a specific audience and identifies its preferences, quirks, behavior, attitudes, needs, or requirements. A recruitment brochure for a computer consulting firm has this headline on the cover:

> Introducing a unique career opportunity only a few dozen
> computer professionals in the country will be able to take
> advantage of this year.…

The headline is effective because it focuses on the prospects (information systems professionals) and one of their main concerns in life (their careers), rather than the consulting firm and its history, as most such brochures do.

Write from the customer's point of view. Instead of beginning with something like "Introducing our Guarda-Health Employee Benefits Program," say "At last you can combat the huge health insurance premiums threatening to put your small business out of business."

WEKA Publishing, in a direct-mail package promoting the *Electronics Repair Manual*, a do-it-yourself guide for hobbyists and others who want to repair their own homes and office electronics, uses copy that speaks directly to the personality type of the potential buyer:

> If you're handy…fascinated by electronics and the world of high-tech…are happiest with a tool in your hand…and respond to household problems and broken appliances with a defiant, "I'll do it myself"…then fun, excitement, the thrill of discovery, time and money saved, and the satisfaction of a job well done await you when you preview our newly updated Electronics Repair Manual at no risk for a full 30 days.

A good way to ensure that you are focusing on the prospects and not yourself, your product, or your company, is to address the prospect directly in the copy as "you." For example:

> Dear Health Care Administrator:
>
> You know how tough it is to make a decent profit margin in today's world of managed care…and how the HMOs and other plans are putting even more of a squeeze on your margins to fill their own already-swelling coffers.
>
> But what you may not be aware of are the techniques health care providers nationwide are using to *fight back*…and get paid every dollar they deserve for the important work they do.

This direct-mail copy, which successfully launched a new publication, works because it focuses on the prospects and their problems (making money from their health care businesses), and not on the publication—its features or columns—or its editors.

Copy that fails to focus on the prospect often does so because the copywriter does not understand the prospect. If you are writing to metal shop managers, attend a metalworking trade show, read a few issues of the trade publications they subscribe to, and interview some of these prospects in person or over the phone. Study focus group transcripts, attend live focus group sessions, or even accompany salespeople on sales calls to these prospects. The better you understand your target audience, the more you have a feel for the way they think and what they think about, and the more effectively you can target copy that speaks to those concerns.

Element 3. Stress benefits.

Although your prospects may be interested in both the features and the benefits of your product or service, it is almost never sufficient to discuss features only.

Virtually all successful copy discusses benefits. Copy aimed at a lay audience primarily stresses benefits, mentioning features mainly to convince the prospects that the product can in fact deliver the benefits promised in the ad.

Copy aimed at specialists often gives equal play to features and benefits, or may even primarily stress features. But whenever a feature is described, it must be linked to a customer benefit it provides. Buyers not only want to know what the product is and what it does, they want to know how it can help them achieve the benefits they want—such as saving money, saving time, making money, looking better, feeling fitter, or being happier.

In copy for technical products, clearly explaining the feature makes the benefit more believable. Don't just say a product has greater capacity; explain what feature of the product allows it to deliver this increased capacity. A brochure for Lucent Technologies' wireless CDMA technology explains:

> CDMA gives you up to 10 times the capacity of analog cellular communication with more efficient use of spectrum.
> Use of a wideband block of radio frequency (RF) spectrum for transmission (1.25 MHz) enables CDMA to support

up to 60 or more simultaneous conversations on a given frequency allocation.

A brochure for a computer consulting firm tells corporate information systems (IS) managers how working with outside consultants can be more cost effective than hiring staff, thus saving money:

> When you augment your IS department with our staff consultants, you pay our staff consultants only when they work for you. If the need ends tomorrow, so does the billing. In addition, various studies estimate the cost of hiring a new staff member at 30% to 60% or more of the annual salary (an executive search firm's fee alone can be 30% of the base pay). These expenditures are 100% eliminated when you staff through us.

In an ad for a software package that creates letterheads using a PC and a laser printer, the copy stresses the benefits of ease, convenience, and cost savings versus having to order stationery from a printer:

> **Now save thousands of dollars on stationery printing costs.**
>
> Every day, law firms struggle with the expense and inconvenience of engraved and preprinted stationery.
>
> Now, in a sweeping trend to cut costs without sacrificing prestige, many are trading in their engraved letterhead for Instant Stationery desktop software from Design Forward Technologies.
>
> With Instant Stationery, you can laser-print your WordPerfect documents and letterhead together on whatever grade of blank bond paper you choose. Envelopes, too. Which means you never have to suffer the cost of expensive preprinted letterhead—or the inconvenience of loading stationery into your desktop printer—ever again.

Element 4. Differentiate yourself from the competition.

Today your customer has more products and services to choose from than ever before. Therefore, to make your product stand out in the buyer's mind and convince him or her that it is better than and different from the competition's, you must differentiate it from those other products in your copy. Crispix cereal, for example, is advertised as the cereal that "stays crisp in milk." Post Raisin Bran is advertised as the only raisin bran having "two scoops of raisins" in each box of cereal. A cookie maker recently ran a campaign promoting "1,000 chips" in every bag of chocolate chip cookies.

Companies that make a commodity product often differentiate themselves on the basis of service, expertise, or some other intangible. BOC Gases, for example, promotes itself as a superior vendor not because their product is better (they sell oxygen, and oxygen is oxygen), but because of their ability to use oxygen and technology to benefit the customer's business. Here is copy from a brochure aimed at steelmakers:

> An oxygen supplier who knows oxygen and EAF steelmaking can be the strategic partner who gives you a sustainable competitive advantage in today's metals markets. And that's where BOC Gases can help.

If your product is unique within its market niche, stress this in your copy. For example, there are dozens of stock market newsletters, but *IPO Insider* claims to be the only IPO bulletin aimed at the consumer (there are other IPO information services, but these target professional investors and money managers). The subscription promotion for *IPO Insider* says:

> IPO Insider is the only independent research and analysis service in the country designed to help the individual investor generate greater-than-average stock market profits in select recommended IPOs.

Lucent Technologies, the AT&T spin-off, competes with many other companies that manufacture telecommunications network equipment. They differentiate themselves by stressing the tested reliability of their switch, which has been documented as superior to other switches in the industry. One brochure explains:

> The 5ESS-2000 DCS Switch is one of the most reliable digital switches available for wireless systems today. According to the U.S. Federal Communication Commission's (FCC)

ARMIS report, the 5ESS-2000 switch has the least down-
time of any switch used in U.S. networks, exceeding
Bellcore's reliability standards by 200%. With an installed
base of more than 2,300 switches, the 5ESS-2000 Switch
currently serves over 72 million lines in 49 countries.

Element 5. Prove your case.

Element 4 identifies the need for product differentiation. Element 3
indicates the need for substantial benefits to product purchasers. But
these elements cannot stand alone, precisely because they are claims—
claims made in a paid advertisement. Therefore, skeptical consumers
do not usually accept them at face value. Unless you back up your
claims with proof, people won't believe that your product is better,
faster, or cheaper.

IC Systems convinces dentists it is qualified to handle their collections by presenting facts and statistics:

> The nationwide leader in dental-practice collections, IC
> Systems has collected past-due accounts receivables for
> 45,717 dental practices since 1963. Over 20 state dental
> associations recommend our services to their members.

> *IC Systems can collect more of the money your patients owe
> you.* Our overall recovery rate for dental collections is 12.4%
> <u>higher</u> than the American Collectors' Association national
> average of 33.63%. (For many dental practices, we have
> achieved recovery rates even higher!)

BOC Gases tells customers that the gas mixtures they sell in cylin-
ders are accurately blended, and therefore that the composition listed
on the label is what the buyer will find inside the container. They
make this claim credible by explaining their blending and weighing
methodology:

> Each mixture component is weighed into the cylinder on
> a high-capacity, high-sensitivity equal-arm balance hav-
> ing a typical precision of ±10 mg at 95% confidence.
> Balanceaccuracy is confirmed prior to weighing by cali-
> bration with NIST-traceable Class S weights. Electronic

integration of the precision balance with an automated filling system provides extremely accurate mixtures with tight
blend tolerances.

Many stock market newsletters promise big winners that will make
the reader rich if he or she subscribes. Since everyone says it, the statement is usually greeted with skepticism. The newsletter *Gold Stocks
Advisory* combats this skepticism by putting their recent successes right
on the outer envelope and at the top of page one of their sales letter:

A SAMPLE OF PAUL SARNOFF'S RECENT HIGH-PROFIT GOLD STOCK PICKS:

Company	Purchase Price	Year High	% Increase/ Time Frame	Potential Profit on 10,000 Shares
Gold Canyon	C70 cents	C$10.50	2793% in 14 months	C$195,500
Coral Gold	C$1.20	C$6.45	438% in 8 months	C$52,500
Bema Gold	C$2.20	C$13.05	439% in 20 months	C$108,500
Jordex	C70 cents	C$3.75	435% in 6 months	C$26,300
Glamis Gold	US$1	US$8.88	788% in 84 months	US$78,800
Barrick Gold	US$4.81	US$32.88	584% in 96 months	US$280,700

The most powerful tool for proving your case is to demonstrate a
good track record in your field, showing that your product or service
is successful in delivering the benefits and other results you promise.
One way to highlight a favorable track record is to include case histories and success stories in your copy. A testimonial from a satisfied
customer is another technique for convincing prospects that you can
do what you say. You can also impress prospects by showing them a
full or partial list of your customers.

Share with readers any results your firm has achieved for an individual customer or group of customers. IC Systems, for example, im-
pressed dentists by telling them that the company collected more than
$20 million in past-due bills over the last two years alone—a number
that creates the perception of a service that works.

Element 6. Establish credibility.

In addition to wanting to know the benefits of the products and services you offer and the results you have achieved, prospective buyers will ask the question, "Who are you?"

In terms of persuasion, the "corporate" story is usually the least important. The prospect is primarily interested in himself and his problems and needs, and interested in your product or service only as a means of solving those problems or filling those needs. The prospect is interested in your company only as it relates to your ability to reliably make, deliver, install, and service the product he or she buys from you or to successfully carry out the service.

Yet, the source of the product or service—the company—is still a factor in influencing purchase decisions. In the early days of personal computing, IBM was the preferred brand—not because IBM necessarily made a superior computer at a better price, but because if something went wrong, IBM could be counted on for fast, reliable, and effective service and support. As PCs became more of a commodity and local computer resellers and stores offered better service, the service and support reputation of IBM became less of an advantage, and their PC sales declined.

Here are some examples of copy in which vendors provide credentials designed to make the consumer feel more comfortable in doing business with them and choosing them over other suppliers advertising similar products and services:

> We guarantee the best technical service and support. I was a compressor service technician at Ingersoll Rand, and in the last 20 years have personally serviced more than 250 compressors at over 80 companies.

> For nearly 100 years, BOC Gases has provided innovative gas technology solutions to meet process and production needs. We have supplied more than 20,000 different gases and gas mixtures—in purities up to 99.99999 percent—to 2 million customers worldwide.

Lion Technology is different. For nearly two decades, we have dedicated ourselves 100% to training managers, engineers, and others in environmental compliance-related subjects. Since 1989, our firm has conducted more than 1,400 workshops nationwide on these topics.

You'll find some of Paul Sarnoff's fundamental research in precious metals summed up in his more than 60 best-selling books including *Silver Bulls* and *Trading with Gold*. Paul's unique blending of solid research, combined with an unprecedented record of success in picking gold stocks, may have been what moved one *New York Times* reporter to dub him "the dean of commodities researchers."

Credentials you can list in your copy include year founded, number of years in business, number of employees, annual revenues, number of locations, number of units sold, patents and product innovations, awards, commendations, publications, membership and participation in professional societies, seals of approval, agency ratings, independent survey results, media coverage, number of customers, and in-house resources (financial, technological, and human).

Element 7. Build value.

It's not enough to convince prospects you have a great product or a superior service. You must also show them that the value of your offer far exceeds the price you are asking for it. You may have the best widget in the $100 to $200 price range of medium-size widgets, but why should the prospect pay $200 for your widget when another brand is sold for half the price? One argument might be the lower total cost of ownership. Your widget may cost more initially, but in the long run it will save and make your firm money through its greater reliability and performance.

Stress cost of ownership versus cost of purchase. The purchase price is not the only cost of owning something. There are the costs of maintenance, support, repair, refurbishment, operation, and, when something wears out, replacement. Therefore, the product that costs the least to buy may not actually cost the least to own; in fact, it can be the most expensive.

Here's a simple example. You need to buy a photocopier for your home office. Copier A costs $900. Copier B costs $1,200. The features are essentially the same, and the reputations of the brands are comparable. Both have an expected lifetime of 120,000 copies. Most people would say, "Everything's the same except price, so buy Copier A and save $300." Copier A compares itself feature for feature with Copier B, and runs an ad with the headline, "Copier A vs. Our Competition…We Can Do Everything They Can Do…at 25% Off the Price."

But you are the copywriter for the maker of Copier B. You ask them what it costs to make a copy. Their cost per copy is 2 cents. You investigate Copier A, and find out that the toner cartridges are more expensive, so that the cost per copy is 4 cents. You can now advertise copies at "half the cost of our competitor."

What's more, a simple calculation shows that if Copier B is 2 cents a copy cheaper, and you use the machine to make 120,000 copies, your savings over the life of the machine is $2,400. Therefore, an investment in Copier B pays you back eight times the extra $300 it cost to buy. This is additional ammunition you can use in your copy to establish that purchase price is not the ultimate factor determining cost, and that Copier B offers a greater overall value to the buyer.

If your product costs slightly more up front but actually saves money in the long run, stress this in your ad copy. Everyone knows that the cheapest product is not necessarily the best buy; corporate buyers are becoming increasingly concerned with the cost of ownership. Only government business, which is awarded based on sealed proposals and bids, seems to still focus solely on the lowest purchase price—and even that is slowly changing.

The key to establishing value is to convince the prospects that the price you ask is "a drop in the bucket" compared with the money your product will make or save them, or the other benefits it delivers. Some examples:

> What would you do if the EPA assessed a $685,000 fine against your company for noncompliance with environmental regulations you *weren't even aware existed?*
>
> ———————
>
> *Now get the special 50th Anniversary Edition of* PERRY'S CHEMICAL ENGINEERS' HANDBOOK *for only $4.97*

> *(list price: $129.50) with your No-Risk Trial Membership in*
> *McGraw-Hill's Chemical Engineers' Book Club.*

Another way to establish value is to compare the cost of your product with more expensive products or services that address the same basic need:

> The cost of The Novell Companion, including the 800+ page reference binder and NetWare utilities on diskette, is normally $89 plus $6.50 for shipping and handling. <u>This is less than a NetWare consultant would charge to advise you for just one hour.</u> Yet, The Novell Companion is there to help you administer and manage your network, year after year.

If your product or service is used over a period of time, as most are, you can reduce the "sticker shock" that comes with quoting a high up-front price by showing the cost over the extended usage period. For instance, a life insurance policy with an annual premium of $200 "gives your loved ones protection for just 55 cents a day." The latter seems more affordable, although the two prices are equivalent.

Element 8. Close with a call to action.

Copy is written to bring about a change—that is, to cause prospects to change their opinion, attitude, beliefs, purchasing plans, brand preferences, or current buying patterns.

To effect this change, your copy must be specific about the action prospects should take if they are interested in what you've said and want to take advantage of your offer, or at least find out more about it. Tell them to clip and mail the coupon, call the toll-free phone number, visit your Web site, come to your store, request a free estimate. If you don't specify what the next step is in your copy, few people will take it. Some examples:

> When you call, be sure to ask how you can get a FREE copy of our new audiocassette, *How to Get Better Results from Your Collection Efforts.* In just 7 minutes of listening, you'll discover at least half a dozen of the techniques IC Systems uses—and you can use, too—to get more people to pay what they owe you.

For a complimentary copy of the SECRETS OF BUILD-ING A WORLD-CLASS WEB SITE audiocassette, complete and mail the survey enclosed or fax it today to 1 888 FAX 2IBM (1 888 329 2426).

Put BOC's quality gas solutions to work in your plant— starting today.

Think it's time to talk with a gas supplier that really knows your business and has real solutions to your problems? Call your BOC Gases representative today. Or visit our Web site at http://www.boc.com.

CHAPTER TWO
Headlines

In today's environment of "information overload," you must work harder than ever to get your ad or commercial noticed. Newspapers, magazines, television, radio, the World Wide Web, and work-related reading material are all competing for your audience's attention.

In all forms of advertising, the *first impression*—the first thing that is seen, read, or heard—can mean the difference between success and failure. If the first impression is boredom or irrelevancy, the ad will not attract your prospect. But if the copy offers news or helpful information or promises a reward for paying attention, it is well on its way to persuading the reader to buy your product.

What, specifically, is this "first impression"? In a print advertisement, it is the headline and the visual; in a brochure, it's the cover. The first few seconds of a radio or TV commercial are the most critical. For a direct-mail package, the copy on the outer envelope or the first few sentences in the letter must grab the reader immediately. In a press release, it's the lead paragraph that counts. On a Web site, the opening screen of the home page is most critical. For newsletters, it's the masthead and the headline of the main cover story. And in sales presentations, it's the first few slides or flip charts, or the first few words you say.

Here are some tips for making your headlines more effective and compelling.

1. Appeal to your audience's self-interest.

Customers want products that satisfy their needs—and their budgets. Good copywriters recognize this fact, and put sales appeals—not cute, irrelevant gimmicks and wordplay—in their headlines. They know that when readers browse ad headlines they want to know: "What's in it for me?" The effective headline tells the reader: "Hey, stop a minute! This is something you want!"

A classic appeal to self-interest is the headline "How to Win Friends and Influence People," from an ad for the Dale Carnegie book of the same name. The headline promises that you will make friends and be able to persuade others if you read the ad and order the book.

A recent ad for Kraft Foods appeals to the homemaker with the headline "How to Eat Well for Nickels and Dimes." If you are interested in good nutrition for your family but must watch your budget carefully, this ad speaks directly to your needs.

The headline for a Hellmann's Real Mayonnaise ad hooks us with the question "Know the Secret to Moister, Richer Cake?" We are promised a reward—the secret to great cake—in return for reading the copy.

Each of these headlines offers a benefit to the consumer: a reward for reading the copy. And each promises specific, helpful information in return for the time invested in reading the ad and the money spent to buy the product.

2. Get your audience's attention.

We've already seen how headlines get attention by appealing to the consumer's self-interest. Here are a few more examples of this type of headline:

> Give Your Kids a Fighting Chance (Crest)
>
> Why Swelter Through Another Hot Summer? (GE air conditioners)
>
> For Deep-Clean, Oil-Free Skin, Noxzema Has the Solution (Noxzema moisturizer)

Another effective attention-getting strategy is to alert the reader to something new. Headlines often use words and phrases such as *new, discover, introducing, announcing, now, it's here, at last,* and *just arrived.*

> This New Sensational Video Can Give You Thin Thighs Starting Now! (exercise videotape)

> Discover Our New Rich-Roasted Taste (Brim decaffeinated coffee)
>
> Introducing New Come 'n Get It. Bursting with New Exciting 4-Flavor Taste. (Come 'n Get It dog food)

If you can legitimately use the word *free* in your headline, do so. *Free* is the most powerful word in the copywriter's vocabulary. Everybody wants to get something for free.

For example, the headline of a *TV Guide* insert for Silhouette Romance novels reads, "Take 4 Silhouette Romance Novels FREE (A $9.80 Value)...And Experience The Love You've Always Dreamed Of." In addition, the word *free* is used a total of 23 times in the body copy and on the reply card.

Other powerful attention-getting words and phrases include *how to, why, sale, quick, easy, bargain, last chance, guarantee, results, proven,* and *save.* Do not avoid these because other copywriters use them so frequently. Other copywriters use them because *they work.*

Headlines that offer the consumer guidance are also attention-getters. The information promised in the headline can be given in the copy or in a free booklet the reader can send for. Some examples:

> Free New Report on 67 Emerging Growth Stocks (Merrill Lynch)
>
> Three Easy Steps to Fine Wood Finishing (Minwax Wood Finish)

3. Use appropriate appeals.

Many advertisers try to get attention with headlines and gimmicks that don't promise the reader a benefit or are not related to the product. One industrial manufacturer featured a photo of a bikini-clad woman in several of their ads, along with an offer of a reprint of the photo to readers who clipped the coupon and requested a brochure on the manufacturer's equipment.

Does this sort of approach get attention? Yes, but not attention that leads to a sale or to real interest in the product. Attention-getting for attention-getting's sake attracts the curious, but is not compelling to serious customers.

When you write a headline, get attention by selecting an important customer benefit and presenting it in a clear, bold, dramatic fashion. Avoid headlines and concepts that are cute, clever, and titillating but irrelevant. They may generate some interest, but they do not sell.

Here are some headlines that lure the prospect in an appropriate, relevant manner designed to generate interest *and* response:

> **Now save thousands of dollars on stationery printing costs...**
> *With Instant Stationery, you'll never buy costly printed stationery again!*

> WALT DISNEY'S <u>MAID</u>
> built a $9 million stock portfolio
> using the simple technique
> inside this envelope!

> Now get business and accounting software
> equivalent to the systems run by
> <u>multi-billion dollar conglomerates</u>...
> ...at a tiny <u>fraction</u> of the cost
> Fortune 500 companies have paid.

4. Speak directly to your audience.

Use your headline to define your audience and appeal to your target market. This will increase readership and response while cutting down on "tire-kicker" type inquiries.

For instance, if you are selling life insurance to people over age 65, there is no point in writing an ad that generates inquiries from younger people. In the same way, an ad for a $55,000 sports car should make it obvious that this is for rich folks only. You don't want to waste time answering inquiries from people who can't afford the product.

The headline can zero in on the ideal audience for your ad and screen out those readers who are not potential customers. A good headline for the life insurance ad might read, "To Men and Women Over 65 Who Need Affordable Life Insurance Coverage." One possible headline for the sports car ad is, "For Those Ready for the Ultimate in a Luxury Sports Car..."

Here are a few more headlines that do a good job of selecting the right audience for the product:

> We're Looking for People to Write Children's Books. (The Institute of Children's Literature)

> ———

> A Message to All Charter Security Life Policyholders of Single Premium Deferred Annuities (Charter Security Life Insurance)

> ———

> Is Your Electric Bill Too High? (utility ad)

Do not explicitly identify the audience in the headline if the nature of the product or service makes it unnecessary or redundant. A recent headline in the New York *Daily News*, "Penile Enlargement for Men Only," would have been stronger with the simpler and more direct headline "Penile Enlargement." Another ad offered "Maternity Clothes for Pregnant Women." Who else would wear them?

5. Deliver a meaningful message.

According to David Ogilvy, author of *Ogilvy on Advertising*, four out of five readers will read the headline and skip the rest of the ad. If this is the case, it pays to make a complete statement in your headline; that way, the ad can do some selling to the 80 percent of the readers who read only the headline. Here are a few headlines that deliver complete messages:

> Caught Soon Enough, Early Tooth Decay Can Actually Be Repaired by Colgate! (Colgate toothpaste)

> ———

> Gas Energy Inc. Cuts Cooling and Heating Costs Up to 50% (Hitachi chiller-heaters)

> ———

> You Can Make Big Money in Real Estate Right Now (Century 21)

Ogilvy recommends that you include the selling promise and the brand name in the headline, although many effective headlines don't. But if you suspect that most of your prospects won't bother to read the copy underneath, then include the product name in the headline.

6. Draw the reader into your body copy.

A few product categories—liquor, soft drinks, and fashion, for example—can be sold with an attractive photo, a powerful headline, and a minimum of words. But many items—automobiles, computers, books, records, telephones—require that the reader be given a lot of information. That information appears in the body copy, and for the ad to be effective, the headline must compel the reader to read this copy.

To draw readers into the body copy, you must arouse their curiosity. You can do this with humor or by being provocative or mysterious. You can ask a question, promise a reward, give news, or offer useful information.

A sales letter promoting an employee benefits plan was mailed to business managers. The headline of the letter was, "When an employee gets sick, how long does it take your company to recover?" Naturally, managers wanted to read on and find out about the benefits of the plan.

The headline of an ad for a facial lotion reads, "The $5 Alternative to Costly Plastic Surgery." Readers are lured into the ad to satisfy their curiosity about what this inexpensive alternative might be. The headline would not be as successful if it said, "$5 Bottle of Lotion Is an Inexpensive Alternative to Costly Plastic Surgery."

PFS Software begins its ad with the headline, "If You're Confused About Buying a Personal Computer, Here's Some Help." If you *are* confused about a computer, you will want to read the ad to get the advice offered in the headline.

7. Use direct headlines when writing about straightforward offers and high-interest products.

Direct headlines state the selling proposition in straightforward terms, without wordplay, hidden meanings, or puns. "Pure Silk Blouses—30 Percent Off" is a headline that's about as direct as you can get. Most retailers use newspaper ads with direct headlines to announce sales and bring customers into the store.

Direct headlines work best when the offer is simple and attractive and the product is in demand. For example, people know what silk blouses are, and 30 percent off is a clear, understandable offer.

Another example: A pet store in New York City was losing business because of the manager's disagreeable personality. The owner found out and fired him. The next day employees put up a sign in the store window that read, "The Nasty Old Man Is Gone." The new manager reported an immediate increase in business.

8. Express your sales proposition in a fresh and compelling way.

With products that are unfamiliar, not in demand, and not inherently desirable or fascinating, you must work even harder to capture the imagination. This can be done with a headline that expresses the main thought with a twist or in a fresh or compelling way. Such a headline makes its point in a roundabout way. It arouses curiosity, and the questions it raises are answered in the body copy.

For example, the headline of an ad for an industrial mixing device reads, "Ten Million to One, We Can Mix It." At first this sounds like a wager—the company is betting ten million to one that its mixer can handle your mixing applications. But when you read the copy, you discover that the real significance of "ten million to one" is the mixer's ability to mix two fluids, one of which is as much as ten million times thicker than the other. The headline has a double meaning, and you have to read the copy to get the real message.

9. Inject news into your headline.

If you have news about your product, announce it in the headline. This news can be the introduction of a new product, an improvement of an existing product ("new, *improved* Bounty"), or a new application for an old product. Some examples of headlines that contain news:

> The First Transportable Computer Worth Taking Anywhere (Apple IIc)

> Finally, a Caribbean Cruise as Good as Its Brochure (Norwegian American Line)

The Norwegian American headline, in addition to containing news, has added appeal because it empathizes with the reader's situation. We've all been disappointed by fancy travel brochures that promise better than they deliver. Norwegian American gains credibility in our eyes by calling attention to this well-known fact.

10. Offer to teach the reader something useful.

Just as in the titles of books and magazine articles, the words *how to* are pure magic in advertising headlines. (There are more than 7,000 books in print with *how to* in their titles.) Some copywriters claim that if you begin with the words *how to,* you can't write a bad headline. They may be right.

How-to headlines offer the promise of solid information, sound advice, and solutions to problems:

> How to Turn a Simple Party into a Royal Ball

> How to Write Better and Faster

> How to Stop Smoking in 30 Days...Or Your Money Back

Whenever you're stuck for a headline, type *how to* on your keyboard, and what follows those words always completes a decent, hardworking headline—good enough to use until something better comes along.

11. Ask a provocative question.

To be effective, the headline must ask a question that the reader can relate to or would like to have answered. Some examples:

> Is Your Pump Costing You More to Operate Than It Should? (Gorman-Rupp pumps)

> Do You Close the Bathroom Door Even When You're the Only One Home? (from a letter selling subscriptions to *Psychology Today*)

> Have You Any of These Decorating Problems? (Bigelow carpets)

Question headlines should always focus on the reader's self-interest, curiosity, and needs—and *not* on the advertiser's. A typical self-serving question headline used by many companies reads something like, "Do You Know What the XYZ Company Is Up to These Days?" The reader's response is "Who cares?" and a turn of the page.

12. Tell customers want you want them to do.

Headlines that directly tell prospects to buy a product, visit a dealer, or take another action are called *command headlines.* Command headlines generate sales by calling for immediate action. Here are some examples:

> Make Your Most Valuable Information Worthless (Destroyit paper shredders)
>
> Try Burning This Coupon (Harshaw Chemical Company)
>
> Put a Tiger in Your Tank (Esso)
>
> Aim High. Reach for New Horizons. (Air Force recruitment)

The first word in the command headline is a verb demanding action on the part of the reader.

13. Use the "reason why" approach.

One easy and effective way of writing body copy is to list the sales features of your product in a simple 1-2-3 fashion. If you write the body this way, you can use a reason-why headline to introduce the list. Examples of reason-why headlines:

> 7 Reasons Why You Should Join the American Institute of Aeronautics and Astronautics
>
> 120 to 4,000 Reasons Why You Should Buy Your Fur During the Next Four Days
>
> 11 Reasons Why ProtoTech Should Make Your Next Prototype

Reason-why headlines need not actually contain the phrase *reasons why.* Other introductory phrases such as *6 ways, 7 steps,* and *here's how* work just as well.

14. Put the headline in quotation marks.

In a testimonial advertisement, your customers do your selling for you. An example of a testimonial is the Publishers Clearing House commercial in which past winners tell us how they won big prize money in the sweepstakes.

Testimonials work because they offer *proof* that a product or service satisfies its customers. In print-ad testimonials, the copy is written as a direct quote from the customer, who is often pictured in the ad.

When writing testimonial copy, allow the customer's own words to make the point. A natural, conversational tone adds believability to the testimonial, so try not to edit the quote too much.

The most important part of the testimonial ad is the headline. Headlines in quotation marks attract more attention than those without. In fact, quotation marks increase readership so sharply that it is desirable to use them even if the headline is not a direct quotation and the ad is not a testimonial ad. Simply put quotations around the headline. For example, instead of:

Get all the money you need for your business—guaranteed.

use:

"Get all the money you need for your business—guaranteed."

Placing headlines and body copy in quotation marks when they are not actual quotes is a technique known as the *unattributed testimonial*. It is the advertisers, not their clients, who are saying the words in quotation marks, and they are, in effect, quoting themselves in their own copy. Tricky, but perfectly ethical. And perfectly legal.

15. Make headlines and visuals work together.

To rely on words alone to do your selling is to use only half the tools at your disposal. Visuals can work with headlines to create a unified sales approach more powerful than either one alone.

The visual you use should be a photograph or drawing that communicates the main idea stated in the headline. Advertising agency professionals often refer to the combination of headline and visual as the ad *concept*. The concept communicates the gist of your sales pitch in one quick take. "Every good ad should be able to stand as a poster," writes Alastair Crompton in his book, *The Craft of Copywriting*. "The reader should never have to dip into the small print in order to understand the *point* of the story." Interested prospects will dip into the body copy if the concept is sufficiently compelling.

Even if the reader never looks at the body copy, the headline and visual should communicate the basic selling message on their own. An example is an ad for diapers. The visual is a rear view of a baby sitting, with her bottom diapered. The headline: "To Be a Great Parent, You've Got to Start at the Bottom."

Simple visuals are often the best. "We tested two different mail order ads selling a collector's reproduction of a watch originally manufactured in the 1920s," said Will Stone of the Hamilton Watch Company. "One ad used a large, dramatic photo showing the watch against a plain background. The other visual had less emphasis on the product and focused on a scene depicting the 'roaring twenties' period during which the watch was originally made. It showed flappers and a 1920s car. The ad with the straight product photo—'product as hero'—generated three times as many sales as the other version."

Even in today's highly styled visual world of MTV, CD-ROMs, and Sega Genesis, visuals that simply show the product or illustrate some aspect of its use are often more effective than creative or unusual concepts that can actually hide what you are selling, thus reducing the ad's persuasiveness.

Avoid *borrowed interest* visuals. These are visuals that have nothing to do with your product, and therefore need to be linked to the copy with a transition headline that artificially ties in the subject of the picture with the subject of the ad. A typical example: A corporate ad for a large steelmaker features a Leroy Nieman–like drawing of a quarterback throwing a football, and the headline says, "In Manufacturing, XYZ Steel Helps You Win the Game."

Use visuals that appeal to your prospects. Mothers like pictures of babies. Cat owners are attracted to pictures of cats. Coin collectors want to look at coins, stamp collectors at stamps.

The best visuals not only catch the reader's eye but complement the theme of the headline. The headline of an ad for RCA Communications reads: "Announcing a Painless Cut in Defense Spending." It's a simple, effective statement that stands on its own. But by adding the visual of a shrinking army telephone photographed against a backdrop of an American flag, we immediately learn that lower phone bills are the cause of the cut in defense spending.

The headline in Crown Royal's ad, "How to Turn a Simple Party into a Royal Ball," promises to tell us how to add a touch of class to an ordinary get-together. But instead of having to read copy to find the answer, a picture of the product tells us immediately that Crown Royal Whiskey makes parties special. Color photography showing the whiskey in glasses of fine crystal emphasizes the product's quality.

In an ad for Diamond Walnuts, the main photo shows a luscious piece of walnut cherry cake; the headline asks, "What Nut Did This?" For a second you wonder why the advertiser would call anyone a nut for baking a cake; when you look at the secondary photo (a bag of Diamond Walnuts) and the body copy underneath, you see that the "nut" that made the cake look so good was the Diamond shelled walnut. The copy is simply the recipe for the cake. This concept is a nice blend of an arresting headline and visual combined with informative body copy. Again, the headline is a pun, but it works because the pun is relevant to the sales message.

By now you get the picture (no pun intended!): A headline and visual that work well together can greatly increase your ad's attention-getting power.

16. Avoid being clever for the sake of being clever.

Creativity should be used to gain attention and interest in a manner that promotes the product. Your goal is to sell something. If you entertain while doing it, fine, but the entertainment should a means to the end, not the end itself. Showmanship, clever phrases, and ballyhoo do not, by themselves, make for a good headline and can actually end up obscuring your point. Creating headlines that are wonderfully clever is worthwhile only if the cleverness enhances the selling message and makes it more memorable. If you have to choose between being clever and obscure or simple and straightforward, we advise you to be the latter. You may not win any advertising awards, but at least you'll sell some merchandise.

Be careful of wording that can give an unintended meaning to your headline. A recent newspaper ad headline proclaimed, "Supreme Adult

Organ." Only after a closer reading did it become clear the ad was for keyboard instruments.

Jim Alexander, president of Alexander Marketing Services, a Michigan-based ad agency, is a firm believer that headlines should sell:

We believe in dramatizing a product's selling message with flair and excitement. Those are important ingredients of good salesmanship in print. But simple statements and plain-Jane graphics often make powerful ads.

For example, the headline "Handling Sulfuric Acid" might sound dull or uncreative to you. To a chemical engineer who's forever battling costly corrosion, that simple headline implies volumes. And makes him want to read every word of the problem-solving copy that follows.

So before we let our clients pronounce an ad dull, we first ask them, "Dull to whom?" Dull to you, the advertiser? Or dull to the reader, our potential customer? It's easy to forget that the real purpose of an ad is to communicate ideas and information about a product. Too many ads are approved because of their entertainment value. That's a waste of money.

CHAPTER THREE
Body Copy

An article in the *Harvard Business Review* described experiments designed to measure advertising effectiveness. The experiments showed, not surprisingly, that advertising is most effective when it is easy to understand. Therefore, you sell more merchandise when you write clear copy.

It sounds obvious. But in practice, many advertisements don't communicate as effectively as they could. An article in *U.S.A. Today* pointed out that 80 years ago, 98 percent of U.S. colleges required students to take at least one course in English composition. Today, almost two-thirds of the colleges have eliminated this requirement. No wonder so many college graduates write so poorly!

Being overly clever for the sake of being clever is a major cause of confusing copy. So are lengthy sentences, clichés, big words, not getting to the point, a lack of specifics, technical jargon, overuse of superlatives, and poor organization. The following tips will help you avoid these evils and write copy that gets your message across to the reader.

1. Put the reader first.

When you write, think about your readers. Ask yourself: Will my readers understand what I have written? Will they know the special terminology I have used? Does my copy tell them something important, new, or useful? If I were the reader, would this copy persuade me to buy the product?

One technique to help you write for the reader is to address the reader directly as *you* in the copy—just as we are writing to you in this book. Copywriters call this the *you-orientation*. Flip through any magazine, and you'll see that 90 percent of the ads contain the word *you* in the body copy.

The left-hand column below shows examples of copy written from the advertiser's point of view. The right-hand column shows the copy revised toward a you-orientation.

Advertiser-Oriented Copy	Reader-Oriented Copy
Bank Plan is the state of the art in user-friendly, sophisticated financial software for small business accounts receivable, accounts payable, and general ledger applications.	Bank Plan can help you: Balance your books. Manage your cash flow. And keep track of customers who haven't paid their bills. Best of all, the program is easy to use—no special training is required.
The objective of the daily cash accumulation fund is to seek the maximum current income that is consistent with low capital risk and the maintenance of total liquidity.	The cash fund gives you the maximum return on your investment dollar with the lowest risk. And you can take out as much money as you like—whenever you like.
To cancel an order, return the merchandise to us in its original container. Upon receipt of the book in good condition, we will inform our Accounting Department that your invoice is canceled.	If you're not satisfied with the book, simply return it to us and tear up your invoice. You won't owe us a cent. What could be fairer than that?

Make your copy interesting. Generate enthusiasm for the product by telling a story, disseminating news, and showing how your product will improve the consumer's life. Remember, you can't bore people into buying your product.

Don't talk about yourself. Don't tell the readers what you did, what you achieved, what you like or don't like. That's not important to them. What's important to them is what *they* like, what *they* need, what *they* want. Make sure your copy discusses facts that are relevant to the reader's self-interest.

2. Carefully organize your selling points.

The Northwestern National Bank in Minneapolis wanted to know if their customers read booklets mailed to them by the bank. So they included an extra paragraph in a booklet mailed to customers. This extra paragraph, buried in 4,500 words of technical information, offered a $10 bill to anyone who asked for it. *Not a single customer asked for the money.*

Obviously, the organization of your material affects the response to it. If the bank had put "$10 is yours free, just for the asking!" on the brochure cover and on the outside of the mailing envelope, many customers would have responded to the offer.

When you write your copy, you must carefully organize the points you want to make. In an ad, you might have one primary sales message ("This car gets good mileage") and several secondary messages ("roomy interior," "low price," "$500 rebate"). The headline states the main selling proposition, and one or more opening paragraphs expand on it. Secondary points are covered in the second half of the ad. If the copy is lengthy, each secondary point can get a separate heading or number.

The organization of your selling points depends on their relative importance, the amount of information you give the reader, and the type of copy you are writing (display ad, letter, commercial, or press release).

An organizational scheme used by many clergy members, seminar leaders, and professional speakers for oral presentations is: "Tell them what you're going to tell them. Tell them. And then tell them. And then tell them what you told them." The speaker first gives an overview of the presentation, covers the important points in sequence, and then briefly summarizes these points. Listeners, unlike readers, cannot refer to a printed page to remind them of what was said, and these overviews and summaries help the audience learn and remember.

Before you create an ad or mailer, write down your sales points. Organize them in a logical, clear, persuasive fashion. Present them in this order when you write your copy. Then make sure the copy flows smoothly from point to point.

3. Divide the copy into short sections.

If the content of your ad can be organized as a series of sales points, you can cover each point in a separate section of copy. This isn't necessary in short ads of 150 words or less. But as the length increases, copy becomes more difficult to read. Breaking the text into several short sections makes it easier to read.

What's the best way to divide the text into sections? Use the most appropriate technique:

- If you have a series of sections where one point follows logically from the previous point, or where the sales points are listed in order of importance, use numbers.

- If there is no particular order of importance or logical sequence between the sales points, use bullets, asterisks, or dashes to set off each new section.

- If you have a lot of copy in each section, use headings (as we've done in this book). Headings are especially effective in sales brochures, copy-heavy full page ads, and direct mail letters of two pages or longer.

Long, unbroken blocks of type intimidate readers. A page filled with a solid column of tiny type says, "This is going to be boring!" If you've used headings and the individual sections are long, use subheads to break up them up. Break long paragraphs into shorter paragraphs. A paragraph of five sentences can usually be broken into two or three shorter paragraphs by finding places where a new thought or idea is introduced and beginning the new paragraph with that thought. You can also allow extra space between paragraphs to avoid a dense look.

4. Use short sentences.

Short sentences are easier to read than long sentences. All professional writers—newspaper reporters, publicists, magazine writers, copywriters—are taught to write in crisp, short, snappy sentences. Long sentences tire and puzzle your readers. By the time they get to the end of a lengthy sentence, they don't remember what was at the beginning.

D. H. Menzel, coauthor of *Writing a Technical Paper,* conducted a survey to find the best length for sentences in technical papers. He found that sentences of more than 43 words were difficult for readers to get through. And the consumer has far less patience with wordiness and run-on sentences than does the scientist studying an important report.

Rudolf Flesch, best known for his books *Why Johnny Can't Read* and *The Art of Plain Talk,* says the best average sentence length for business writing is 14 to 16 words. He adds that 20 to 25 words is passable, but above 40 words the writing becomes unreadable.

Because ad writers place a premium on clarity, their sentences are even shorter than Flesch's recommended 14- to 16-word average. An informal survey of ads for consumer products in national magazines showed the average sentence length was 10 to 12 words. How can you reduce sentence length? There are several techniques. First, break long sentences into two or more separate sentences whenever possible. The sentence

> Today every penny of profit counts and Gorman-Rupp wants your pumps to work for all they're worth.

works better as

> Today every penny of profit counts. And Gorman-Rupp wants your pumps to work for all they're worth.

Another method of breaking a long sentence is to use punctuation to divide it into two parts. Note the difference the punctuation makes in the second sentence in each of these examples:

One purpose is to enable you to recognize and acknowledge the contributions of all of your fellow employees from the company president right down to the newest foreman.	One purpose is to enable you to recognize and acknowledge the importance of all of your fellow employees—from the company president right down to the newest foreman.
The result is presentations that don't do their job and that can make others wonder whether you're doing *yours.*	The result is presentations that don't do their job…and that can make others wonder whether you're doing *yours.*

Copy becomes dull when all the sentences are the same length. To make your writing flow, vary sentence length. Even if you frequently write longer sentences, you can reduce the overall sentence length in your copy by interspersing the occasional short sentence or sentence fragment, as in these examples:

Over 30,000 aerospace engineers have become members. To join them, send your check for $46 with the coupon below.	Over 30,000 aerospace engineers have become members. Join them. Send your check for $46 with the coupon below.

Now, discover the Splint-Lock System, an effective and versatile chairside splinting technique that helps you stabilize teeth quickly, easily, and economically.	Now, discover the Splint-Lock System...an effective and versatile chairside splinting technique that helps you stabilize teeth. Quickly. Easily. And economically.

Sentence fragments—phrases and clauses that are not grammatically complete sentences—can be used to keep your sentences short. And sentence fragments can add drama and rhythm to your copy, as in the following:

> Basic Eye Emphasizer does it all. It's the one eye makeup everyone needs. The only one.

> Not one of the Fortune 1000 companies even comes close to our rate of growth. And no wonder. Computers are the hottest product of the 1990s, with no end to demand in sight.

> It doesn't take much to block the door to success. A flash of an idea that slips your mind. A note that never gets written.

Train yourself to write in crisp, short sentences. When you have finished a thought, stop. Start the next sentence with a new thought. When you edit, you should automatically seek out sentences that can be broken in two.

5. Use simple words.

Simple words communicate more effectively than complex ones. People use big words to impress others, but more often than not those fancy words annoy and distract readers from what the writer is trying to say.

Yet big words persist, perhaps because using inflated language makes the writer or speaker feel important. For example, in one of his sermons, a Unitarian minister said, "If I were God, my goal would be to maximize goodness, not to eternalize evil."

In advertising copy, you are trying to *communicate* with people, not impress them or boost your own ego. Avoid pompous words and fancy phrases. Direct marketing expert Cecil Hoge says the words in your copy should be "like the windows in a storefront. The reader should be able to see right through them and see the product."

Below, the left-hand column lists some big words that have appeared in recent ads, brochures, and articles. The right-hand column gives simpler—and preferable—choices.

Big Word	Substitute Word or Phrase
assist	help
automobile	car
container	bottle, jar, package
diminutive	small
employ	use
facilitate	help
facility	building, factory, warehouse
finalize	finish, complete, conclude
garment	suit, shirt, dress
indicate	tell, say, show
obtain	get
optimum	best
prioritize	set priorities, rank
procure	get
perspiration	sweat
purchase	buy
substantiate	prove
utilize	use
terminate	end, finish
visage	face

Small words are better than big ones whether you're writing to farmers or physicists, fishermen or financiers. While the majority of well-educated people don't resent complex words, simple words are the only words many people understand.

6. Use jargon sparingly.

Industrial and high-tech copy isn't the only writing that uses technical jargon. Here's a sample from a Porsche ad that ran in *Forbes:*

> The 944 has a new 2.5-liter, 4-cylinder, aluminum-silicon alloy Porsche engine—designed at Weissach, and built at Zuffenhausen.
>
> It achieves maximum torque of 137.2 ft-lbs as early as 3000 rpm, and produces 143 hp at 5500 rpm.
>
> The 944 also has the Porsche transaxle design, Porsche aerodynamics, and Porsche handling.

Like many *Forbes* readers, we're not automotive engineers. We didn't know that torque is achieved in ft-lbs, or that 3000 rpm is considered early for achieving it. We know hp is horsepower and rpm revolutions per minute, but we don't know whether 143 hp at 5500 rpm is good, bad, or mediocre.

The point is: Use jargon sparingly when writing to an audience that doesn't speak your special language. Jargon is useful for communicating within a small group of experts. But in copy aimed at outsiders, it can confuse the reader and obscure the selling message.

Computer and data communications professionals, for example, have created a new language: LAN/WAN internetworking, data warehouse, GUI, client/server, dumb terminal, remote node, Intranet. But not everybody knows the vocabulary. A business executive may know the meaning of *software* and *hardware* but not understand terms like *bindery, bandwidth,* and *computer telephony.* And even a customer with a technical background may be baffled by a brochure that refers to *interprocess message buffers, asynchronous software interrupts,* and *four-byte integer data types.* When you use jargon, you risk turning off readers who don't understand the technical shorthand.

Computer experts aren't alone in baffling us with their lingo. Wall Streeters use an alien tongue when they speak of *downside ticks, standstills, sideways consolidation,* and *revenue enhancements.* Hospital administrators, too, have a language all their own: *cost outliers, prospective payments, catchment areas, diagnostic-related groups, ICD-9 codes.*

It usually the advertisers as specialists in their fields, not their copywriters, who more often inflict jargon on readers. One of our clients rewrote some brochure copy so that their storage silo didn't merely "dump" grain—the grain was "gravimetrically conveyed." Another, a manufacturer of dental products, informed us that dental splints did not "keep loose teeth in place"; they "stabilized mobile dentition."

When is it okay to use technical terms and when is it best to express the concept in plain English? Don't use a technical term unless 95 percent or more of your readers will understand it. If you do use terms that are unfamiliar to your readers, define them in your copy.

Don't use a technical term unless it is the best choice. We would use *software* because there is no better way to say it. But instead of using *deplane,* we would just say, "Get off the plane."

Your prospects should not have to figure out what you mean. It is *your* job to say what you mean in plain, simple English. Use short sentences, short paragraphs, small words. Be clear.

7. Be concise.

Good copy is concise. Unnecessary words waste the reader's time, dilute the sales message, and take up space that could be put to better use.

People have more information to absorb today than ever before, and less time to absorb it. Your prospects are in a hurry and have shorter attention spans than they did 10 or 20 years ago. One study reported that in 1968 political election coverage, the length of the average TV sound byte was 42.3 seconds. Today it is less than 8 seconds.

Rewriting is the key to producing concise copy. When you write your first draft, the words sometimes pour out, and you can't help being chatty. In the editing stage, unnecessary words are deleted to make the writing crisp, pointed, and clear.

One copywriter describes her copy as a "velvet slide"—a smooth path leading the prospect from initial interest to final sale. Excess words are bumps and obstacles that block the slide.

Avoid redundancies, run-on sentences, wordy phrases, the passive voice, unnecessary adjectives, and other poor stylistic habits that take up space but add little to meaning or clarity. Edit your writing to remove unnecessary words, phrases, sentences, and paragraphs.

Here are some examples of wordy phrases and how to make them more concise:

Wordy Phrase	Concise Substitute
at first glance	at first
the number 20	20
whether or not	whether
a general principle	a principle
a specific example	an example
he is a man who	he
they managed to use	they used
from a low of 6 to a high of 16	from 6 to 16
a wide variety of different models	a wide variety of models
approximately 17 tons or so	about 17 tons
expert specialists	experts
simple and easy to use	easy to use
can help you	helps
can be considered to be	is
most unique	unique
the one and only	the only
comes to a complete stop	stops
the entire issue	the issue
dull and boring	boring

Wordy Phrase	Concise Substitute
on an annual basis	yearly
in the form of	as
exhibits the ability to	can
as you may or may not know	as you may know
a substitute used in place of	a substitute for
features too numerous to mention	many features
carbon steel, alloy steel, and stainless steel	carbon, alloy, and stainless steel
feminine hygiene products for women	feminine hygiene products
children's toys	toys
where you were born	your birthplace
your own home	your home
a product that you can use	a product you can use

Tell your story in as few words as possible. When you are finished, stop.

8. Be specific.

Advertising persuades us by giving specific information about the product being advertised. The more facts you include in your copy, the better. Copywriters who don't bother to dig for specifics produce vague, weak, meaningless copy.

"If those who have studied the art of writing are in accord on any one point," write Strunk and White in *The Elements of Style*, "it is this: the surest way to arouse and hold the attention of the reader is by being specific, definite, and concrete. The greatest writers—Homer, Dante, Shakespeare—are effective largely because they deal in particulars and report the details that matter."

When you sit down to write copy, your file of background information should have at least twice as much material as you will end up using in the final version of your ad. When you have a warehouse of facts to choose from, writing copy is easy: You select the most important facts and describe them in a clear, concise, direct fashion.

But when copywriters have little or nothing to say, they fall back on inflated language to fill the page. The words sound nice, but say nothing. And the ad doesn't sell because it doesn't inform.

Here are some examples of vague versus specific copy.

Vague Copy	Specific Copy
He is associated in various teaching capacities with several local educational institutions.	He teaches copywriting at New York University and technical writing at Brooklyn Polytech.
Adverse weather conditions will not result in structural degradation.	The roof won't leak if it rains.
Good Housekeeping is one of the best-read publications in America.	Each month, more than 5 million readers pick up the latest issue of *Good Housekeeping* magazine.

The more specific you are, the less chance your readers will misunderstand you. Some computer users, for example, called a support line to complain that they could not find a key labeled ANY KEY, and that the manual often told them "hit any key." At last report, the computer manufacturer was planning to rewrite the manuals so they specified "hit the RETURN key," eliminating the user's uncertainty.

9. Get to the point.

If the headline is the most important part of an ad, then the lead paragraph is surely the second most important. The lead paragraph, or lead, is what either lures the reader into the text by fulfilling the promise of the headline, or bores the reader with uninteresting and irrelevant information and unnecessary words.

Start selling with the very first line of your lead. If you feel the need to "warm up" as you set your thoughts on paper, do so. But delete

these warm-ups from your final draft. The finished copy should sell from the first word to the last.

Here's an example of copy that fails to get to the point:

AIM HIGH. REACH FOR NEW HORIZONS.

It isn't easy. But reaching for new horizons is what aiming high is all about. Because to reach for new horizons you must have the vision to see things not only as they are, but as they could be.

Copy like this may sound good, but upon closer reading you realize it is full of fluff and says nothing to capture the reader's interest. The ad tries to be dramatic, but the result is empty rhetoric; the copy does not give a clue as to what is being advertised.

This copy appeared in an Air Force recruitment ad. The benefits of joining the Air Force are travel, vocational training, and the chance to fly jets. Why not feature these points right off?

Here, by comparison, is the beginning of a sales letter designed to sell a book and a disk on how to manage computer networks. This letter generated twice as many orders as previous mailings selling the same product:

Now you can <u>maximize</u> network availability—and <u>optimize</u> performance—*all year long...*

New on this FREE diskette—5 powerful software utilities and shareware programs to help you manage your Novell NetWare network more efficiently and easily!

Yours at no extra cost with your no-risk Examination Copy of The Novell Companion—*if you act now.*

Dear LAN Professional:

You're busy. So I'll get right to the point.

The Novell Companion is a unique resource no NetWare LAN professional should be without!

Simply put, it's the most <u>comprehensive</u> and valuable reference work on installing, configuring, administering, and troubleshooting NetWare networks ever available.

> The Novell Companion can help you optimize perfor-
> mance, simplify maintenance, and enhance the reliability
> of your NetWare network…as it has for hundreds of satis-
> fied LAN managers and systems administrators nationwide.

10. Write in a friendly, conversational style.

Ann Landers is one of the most widely read columnists in the country.
Why does she think her column is so popular? "I was taught to write
like I talk," says Ann. "Some people like it." Writing in a conversational
style produces copy that engages your readers.

Conversational tone is especially important in advertising, where
the printed page is an economical substitute for a salesperson. (The
only reason companies advertise is that advertising can reach more
people at less cost than a traveling salesperson can.) A light, conversational style is much easier to read than the stiff, formal prose of business, science, and academia. And when you write simply, you become
the reader's friend. When you write pompously, you become a bore.

For example, IBM's famous Charlie Chaplin ads and commercials
helped make the IBM PC a best-seller. These ads provide a good model
of friendly, helpful, conversational copy. Here's a sample:

> There's a world of information just waiting for you. But to
> use it, study it, enjoy it and profit from it, you first have to
> get at it.
> _____
> Yet the facts can literally be right at your fingertips—
> with your own telephone, a modem and the IBM Personal
> Computer.

Note the use of colloquial expressions ("a world of information,"
"at your fingertips") and the informal language ("just waiting for you,"
"you first have to get at it"). IBM seems to want to help us on a person-
to-person level, and their copy has the sound of one friend talking to
another. But here's how the copy might read if written in strictly technical terms:

> Thousands of databases may be accessed by individuals.
>
> These databases provide information for business, educa-
> tional, and leisure activities.

To access these databases from your home, a telephone, modem, and IBM Personal Computer are required.

See the difference? When you write copy, use conversational tone to make your ads glow with warmth, as IBM's do.

How do you go about it? An article in the *Wall Street Journal* recommends this simple test for conversational tone: "As you revise, ask yourself if you would ever say to your reader what you are writing. Or imagine yourself speaking to the person instead of writing."

A client of ours once wrote a sales letter that began, "Enclosed please find the literature you requested." We asked him, "If you were handing this envelope to me instead of mailing it, what would you say?"

He thought a minute. "Well, I'd say, 'Here is the information you asked for' or 'I've enclosed the brochure you wanted' or something like that."

"Then why not *write* it that way?" we replied.

He did.

And to help you write the way you talk, here are some tips for achieving a natural, conversational style:

- Use pronouns: *I, we, you, they.*

- Use colloquial expressions: *a sure thing, turn on, a rip-off, OK, sick and tired.*

- Use contractions: *you're, I'm, we've, they're, it's, here's.*

- Use simple words.

11. Avoid sexist language.

Sexist language offends a large portion of the population, and you don't sell things to people by getting them angry at you. The day of the advertising man, salesman, and Good Humor man are over. Now it's the advertising *professional, salesperson,* and *Good Humor vendor.*

Handling gender in writing is a sensitive and as yet unresolved issue. Do we change *manpower* to *personpower? Foreman to foreperson? His* to *his/her?*

Fortunately, there are a few techniques for handling the problem:

- Use plurals. Instead of "the doctor receives a report on his patients," write, "the doctors receive reports on their patients."

- Rewrite to avoid reference to gender. Instead of "the manager called a meeting of his staff," write, "the manager called a staff meeting."

- Alternate gender references. Five years ago we used *his* and *he* throughout our copy. Now we alternate *he* with *she* and *his* with *her*. Avoid the awkward constructions *he/she* or *his/her*.

- Create an imaginary person to establish gender. For example: "Let's say Doris Franklin is working overtime. When she punches her time card, she is automatically switched to her overtime pay rate."

- Replace sexist terms with nonsexist substitutes, as in the following list:

Sexist Term	Nonsexist Substitute
anchorman	anchor
advertising man	advertising professional
chairman	chairperson
Englishmen	the English
fireman	firefighter
foreman	supervisor
a man who	someone who
man the exhibit	run the exhibit
man of letters	writer
mankind	humanity
manpower	personnel, staff
manmade	manufactured, artificial
man-hours	work hours
Mrs., Miss	Ms.

Sexist Term	Nonsexist Substitute
newsman	reporter
postman	mail carrier
policeman	police officer
salesman	salesperson
stewardess	flight attendant
self-made man	self-made person
weatherman	meteorologist, weather forecaster
workman	worker

12. Don't be afraid to end your sentence with a preposition.

Writers use a number of stylistic techniques to pack a lot of information into a few short paragraphs of smooth-flowing copy. One technique is to end a sentence with a preposition.

Ending a sentence with a preposition adds to the conversational tone of the copy. And it's a perfectly acceptable technique endorsed by Zinsser, Flesch, Fowler, and most other authorities on modern writing. Some examples:

He's the kind of fellow with whom you'd love to chat.

He's the kind of fellow you'd love to chat with.

———

This is fine china of which you can be proud.

This is fine china you can be proud of.

———

For what are we fighting?

What are we fighting for?

Of course, use your judgment. If ending with a sentence with a preposition sounds awkward, don't do it.

13. Begin sentences with conjunctions.

Beginning a sentence with *and, or, but,* or *for* makes for a smooth, easy transition between thoughts.

Use simple conjunctions instead of more complex connectives. *But* is a shorter, better way of saying *nevertheless, notwithstanding,* and *conversely.* And don't use such cumbersome words and phrases as *furthermore, moreover,* and *equally important* when *and* will do just as well.

Note how conjunctions are effectively used in these examples:

> The first lesson is free. But I can't call you. You have to take the first step.

> We wanted the ECS-100 to incorporate the most advanced vocoder available today. And it does!

> You wouldn't want your friends to die of envy. Or would you?

14. Use graphic and typographic techniques to emphasize words or phrases in copy and to separate thoughts.

If your copy is lengthy, divide it into short sections (as in this book), and consider using headings and subheadings. It makes the copy easier to read.

Using bullets, highlighting, underlining, italics, and boldface can make words and phrases stand out in print advertising and promotion. Many readers skim copy without reading it carefully, so these techniques draw attention to key words, phrases, paragraphs, and selling points.

Of course, these devices should be used sparingly. If you underline every other word in your sales letter, nothing stands out. On the other hand, if you underline only three words in a one-page letter, most prospects will at least read those words.

Here is a list of mechanical techniques copywriters use to call attention to key words and phrases:

bullets

numbered lists

underlining

capital letters

indented paragraphs

boldface type

italics

script

change of type style or size

borders and boxes

color

arrows

yellow highlighting

reverse type (white type on black background)

marginal notes

call-outs

P.S. (in letters)

headings and subheadings

15. Be credible.

People instinctively mistrust advertising and advertising professionals. You must work hard to convince the reader that what you say is true.

One way to establish credibility is to include testimonials from satisfied customers. Another is to provide a demonstration or scientific evidence that proves your claim.

An overlooked technique for getting people to believe you is to *tell the truth*. When you are sincere, your sincerity comes across to your readers and they believe your claims.

You can create strong credibility by including a negative feature or a disadvantage of your product in the copy, not just all the benefits or the advantages. But be selective. Inject one negative only. Do not list all the disadvantages of your product. Choose a flaw that is easily correctable or whose existence doesn't greatly matter to the customer.

Studies have shown that buyers want you to be honest about the limitations of your product as well as the advantages. An example is an ad for a pump company that begins with the headline, "Our pumps are only good for handling certain types of fluids. Know which ones?"

Other techniques for establishing your credibility:

- Talk about the benefits of your product.

- Show the features that enable the product to deliver its benefits.

- Present test results.

- Give a list of satisfied users.

- Use case histories showing how others benefited from the product.

- Show photographs of the product in use.

- Offer an unconditional money-back guarantee of satisfaction.

- Include 90 days of free service or support with the product.

- Quote from favorable reviews or other positive publicity.

CHAPTER FOUR
Power Copywriting Techniques

I n this chapter we go beyond fundamentals to give you some of the techniques America's highest-paid copywriters use to attract attention and increase response to their copy.

Unlike the rules presented in chapter 1, the guidelines in this chapter are not mandatory. Rather, think of them as a "bag of tricks" you can use—tried and tested formulas that work.

Although these are in fact formulas, the overwhelming majority of copywriters—professional ad writers and businesspeople who write their own copy—are unaware of them. So their effectiveness is not diminished through overuse. Using these techniques can add freshness to your copy, making it crisp and compelling, and enabling it to stand out from the crowd.

1. Become a research fanatic.

John Forde of Agora Publishing says the willingness to do research is a key trait that distinguishes good copywriters from mediocre ones.

Before you write copy, study the product—its features, benefits, applications, past performance, and markets. Digging for the facts will pay off, because in business-to-business and consumer advertising, specifics sell.

When you have a file full of facts at your fingertips, writing good copy is easy. You simply select the most relevant facts and describe them in a clear, concise, direct fashion.

But when copywriters don't bother to dig for facts, they fall back on fancy phrases and puffed-up expressions to fill the empty space on the page. The words sound nice, but they don't sell because the copy doesn't inform.

The key to writing great copy is to collect all published background material on your product, your industry, and your market. This material will provide you with the facts you need to write strong, specific selling copy. Even better: Use the product, interview customers, attend sales conferences, and do other first-hand research.

Here is a checklist of materials you should collect from the client and then study before writing your copy. Obviously not every client will be able to provide all of these. But ask for them anyway, and take whatever you can get.

Materials to collect

- Samples of the product
- Tear sheets or reprints of any previous ads
- Files of competitors' ads and sales literature
- Product brochures, data sheets, catalog pages, and any other sales literature describing the product
- Reprints of articles or papers relevant to the product
- Copies of speeches, seminar notes, and PowerPoint presentations about the product made by company personnel for internal or external audiences
- Scripts from slide presentations, videotapes, and films
- Press releases and press kits
- Operator, user, or instruction manuals
- Package copy (labels, boxes, containers, etc.)
- Letters of testimonial from satisfied customers
- Complaint letters
- Completed evaluation forms from seminars, training programs, and consulting services
- Product reviews
- Marketing, advertising, and business plans
- Press clippings

- Direct-mail packages and sales letters
- Company memos and other internal documents describing the product
- Engineer's drawings
- Market research studies
- Focus group transcripts
- Sales figures for past five years (dollar amounts, units sold)
- Annual report or company capabilities brochure (for general company background)
- Back issues of company newsletters
- List of customers, clients, or users
- Names and phone numbers of several people in the company the writer can call for further information on sales and technical aspects of the product
- Names and phone numbers of several customers the writer can call to get the customer's point of view

After reviewing the source material, you will have questions. Arrange with the client to get the answers. These answers may be found in additional source documents you don't have, or you may have to interview various people at the client company to get the facts you need. Interviewing can be done in person, over the phone, or even via fax or e-mail. The questions you should ask include the following:

Questions about the product

- What are the product's features and benefits? (Make a complete list.)
- Which benefit is the most important?
- How is the product different from the competition's? (Which features are exclusive? Which are better than the competition's?)
- If the product isn't different, what attributes can be stressed that haven't been stressed by the competition?

- What technologies does the product compete against?
- What are the applications of the product?
- What industries can use the product?
- What problems does the product solve in the marketplace?
- How is the product positioned in the marketplace?
- How does the product work?
- How reliable, efficient, and economical is the product?
- Who has bought the product and what do they say about it?
- What materials, sizes, and models is it available in?
- How quickly does the manufacturer deliver the product?
- What service and support does the manufacturer offer?
- Is the product guaranteed?

Questions about the potential buyer

- Who will buy the product? (What markets is it sold to?)
- What is the customer's main concern? (quality, price, performance, reliability, efficiency, delivery, service, maintenance)
- What is the character of the typical buyer?
- What motivates the buyer?
- How many different buying influences must the copy appeal to?

If you are writing an ad for a newspaper, magazine, or other periodical, read issues of the publication in which the ad will appear. If you are writing a direct-mail piece, find out what mailing lists will be used and study the data cards, which are written descriptions of each list.

What is the objective or purpose of the copy you are writing? This objective may be one or more of the following: to produce orders, generate inquiries, answer inquiries, qualify prospects, transmit product information, build brand recognition and preference, enhance company image, or instruct the buyer on product usage, applications, or care.

2. Use adjectives.

While many writing instructors tell students to keep the use of adjectives to a minimum, this rule does not hold in advertising. Adjectives allow you to introduce new sales points or reinforce those you've already made without adding sentences or paragraphs. For example, instead of saying "maintenance service" write "low-cost maintenance service." This reinforces the idea that the service is affordable.

The left-hand column lists the subjects written about in recent ads. The right-hand column shows appropriate adjectives that make these subjects sound more impressive and desirable:

software	menu-driven software
methods	effective methods
testing unit	portable testing unit
service	fast, affordable service
manual	comprehensive manual
protocol	industry-standard protocol
communications	digital communications
mixture	precision-blended mixture
line	high-capacity line
cabinets	rugged, weather-resistant cabinets
unit	compact, lightweight unit
system	patented system
generator	EPA-approved generator

3. Tailor your copy to specific market niches.

The most effective sales materials are tightly targeted to specific audiences—for example, an ad for accounting services for nonprofit organizations is better when it is tailored with that particular group in mind, rather than if it simply addresses accounting services in general. The group should be specifically mentioned in the copy.

With so many products and services competing for the consumer's attention, you can differentiate yourself by creating the perception that yours is specifically designed with the reader's unique needs and requirements in mind.

In addition, we are living in an age of specialization, so consumers are looking for products customized for their applications, services tailored to their needs, and suppliers who are knowledgeable about their industry.

In the left-hand column are generic descriptions of products and services from various ads. The right-hand column shows how their appeal can be increased by targeting them to a specific audience:

security	retail and mall security
cigars	fine cigars—for cigar lovers
ski lessons	ski lessons for beginners
life insurance	life insurance for people over 50
furniture	furniture for growing families with kids
computer systems	computer systems for lawyers
industrial gases	industrial gases for refineries
limousine service	corporate limousine service
religious books	Christian books
gifts	gifts for cat lovers
air conditioning	commercial air-conditioning systems

4. Actively solicit testimonials and use them in all your copy.

Using testimonials—quotations from satisfied customers and clients—is one of the simplest and most effective ways of adding punch and power to ad, brochure, and direct-mail copy. Most copywriters are passive about testimonials, using them only when the client provides them. You should become proactive about testimonials, prodding your clients to provide them for every product and service you write about.

Always use real rather than made-up testimonials. Even the most skilled copywriter can rarely invent a testimonial that can match the sincerity and credibility of genuine words of praise from a real customer or client.

If you ask a customer to give you a testimonial, and he or she says, "Sure, just write something and I'll sign it," politely reply, "I appreciate that, but would you mind just giving me your opinions of our product in your own words?" Fabricated testimonials usually sound phony; genuine testimonials invariably have the ring of truth.

Use long testimonials rather than short ones. Many advertisers are hooked on using very short testimonials. For instance:

"…fabulous!…"

"truly funny…thought-provoking…"

"…excellent…wonderful…"

When people see these ultra short testimonials, they suspect that a skillful editing job has masked a comment that was not as favorable as the writer makes it appear. Longer testimonials, say, two or three sentences versus a single word or phrase, come across as more believable. For example:

"Frankly, I was nervous about using an outside consultant. But your excellent service has made me a believer! You can be sure that we'll be calling on your firm to organize all our major sales conferences and other meetings for us. Thanks for a job well done!"

Choose specific, detailed testimonials over general or superlative testimonials. Upon receiving a letter of praise from a customer, your initial reaction might be to read the letter and find the sentences that directly praise the client company or product. With a blue pencil, you might extract the words you think are the kindest, producing a bland bit of puffery such as, "We are very pleased with your product." But testimonials are stronger when they include more of the specific, detailed comments clients have made about *how* the product or service has helped them. After all, the prospects you are trying to sell to may have a problem similar to the one your current customers solved

using the product. If you let your satisfied customers tell the unde-
cided prospects how the company came to their rescue, your current
customers will be helping you make the sale. For instance:

> "We have installed your new ChemiCoat system in each of
> our bottling lines and have already experienced a 25 per-
> cent savings in energy and material costs. Thanks to your
> system, we have now added an additional production line
> with no increase in energy costs. This has increased profits
> 15 percent and already paid back the investment in your
> product. We are very pleased with your product."

Don't try to polish the customer's words so they sound like professional ad copy. Testimonials are usually much more convincing when
they are not edited for style.

When reprinting testimonials, use full attribution. We've all opened
direct-mail packages that contained testimonials from "J. B. in Arizona"
or "Jim S., Self-Made Millionaire." Many readers laugh at such testimonials and think they are phony.

To increase the believability of your testimonials, attribute each
quotation fully. Include the person's full name, city and state, and, if a
business customer, the job title, company, and company location—for
example, "Jim K. Redding, Vice President of Manufacturing, Divmet
Corporation, Fairfield, NJ." People are more likely to believe this sort
of full disclosure rather than testimonials that seem to conceal the iden-
tity of the speaker.

There are two basic ways to present testimonials: You can group
them together in one area of your brochure or ad, or you can scatter
them throughout the copy. (A third method is to combine the two
techniques, having many testimonials in a box or buck slip and a smat-
tering of other testimonials throughout the rest of your copy.)

Both approaches can work well, and the success of the presentation depends in part on the skill of the writer and the specific nature
of the piece. But, all else being equal, the first approach is preferable:
Group all your testimonials and present them as a single block of copy.
This can be done in a box, on a separate page, or on a separate sheet.
When the prospect reads a half dozen or so testimonials one right
after another, they have more impact and power than when they are
separated and scattered throughout the piece.

5. Add interesting or useful information to your copy.

You can increase readership by adding interesting or useful information to your copy. Toss in a few facts, statistics, or buzz words that let prospects know the advertiser understands their industry and their needs. For example:

> It's true: Half the people in the USA don't even *see* a dentist. And they represent a prime prospect for your dental practice.

This fact tells dentists who already know it that you seem to know your business and theirs. Dentists who don't know it appreciate the information and find it thought provoking.

A company that makes training videos recently added short "how-to" articles on training to its catalog. The catalog is better read and has more value for the prospect because of this informational content, which transforms it from a mere product catalog to a valuable resource guide.

If you are offering valuable, interesting, or little-known information in your copy, mention this in your headline or subhead to draw the reader in. Examples:

> Every car wash owner should know these 7 business success secrets. Do you?

> Why haven't satellite dish owners been told these facts?

6. Inject a time element into your copy.

Whenever possible, include a time reference to add immediacy to you copy, as in these examples:

> How to Reduce Your Building Maintenance Costs by 40%

> How to Reduce your Building Maintenance Costs by 40% This Year.

> Read All the Best Business Books in Just 15 Minutes Each

> Read All the Best Business Books of 1997—in Just 15 Minutes Each.

To create a sense of urgency, put a deadline on your offer. The deadline can be a specific date ("Offer expires February 18, 1998") or a specific number of days or weeks ("You must respond within 10 days to get your free gift"). If you cannot give a specific deadline for responding, indicate in the copy that the offer is time limited ("Once this offer expires, it may never be repeated again").

You can make the deadline and the sense of urgency it creates more powerful by giving a legitimate reason for the limitation on the offer, if there is one. For example, if you are selling remainders of a discontinued item, say in your copy, "Only $499 each while they last—limited stock" or "Closeout sale...only 250 units remaining." Real estate ads do this when they tell you that a development is almost completely sold out.

If the reason for your time limitation is unique or unusual, explain it in your copy. This will make the urgency seem more credible. For instance, if you are having a sale on custom-fitted suits and are limited by your tailor's schedule, say:

> These custom suits which normally sell for $1,000 are now on sale for $450 each. But hurry. The limited inventory is available on a first come, first served basis—and our tailor is so booked, we can do only about a dozen fittings a day. So come in NOW!

7. Remove the risk from ordering or inquiring.

Ensure the buyer's satisfaction. Emphasize the advertiser's guarantee in the copy, or, if the advertiser does not explicitly guarantee the product or service, give examples of how they will go out of their way to please the customer.

As a rule, the stronger the guarantee, the more it will increase inquiries and orders. An unconditional money-back guarantee makes consumers feel more at ease than a guarantee with a lot of conditions.

An example of an unconditional guarantee:

> If for any reason you are not 100% satisfied with the product, return it within 60 days for a full refund—no questions asked.

A conditional guarantee:

> If you are not 100% satisfied, return the product in un-
> damaged condition within 60 days for a full refund.

The condition in the second guarantee is "undamaged condition."
Will you accept returns if the customer returns damaged goods and
says the merchandise was damaged when she got it? What if the product gets damaged during the return shipping? The uncertainty caused
by the condition in the guarantee may reduce up-front orders.

A longer guarantee is better than a shorter guarantee. Instead of
a 30-day money back guarantee, offer a 60-day or 90-day money
back guarantee. Having too short a guarantee period—5 or 10 days,
for example—may increase returns by making customers afraid of
being "stuck" with the item if they don't open and examine it in time.

If you are offering a free brochure or catalog to people who respond, state explicitly that the information is free and that there is no
obligation to buy. If you do not intend to follow up in person or over
the phone, add, "No salesperson will call." If you intend to follow up
on the phone but will not send a salesperson unless the prospect re-
quests it, say, "No salesperson will visit."

Part Two
COPYWRITING TASKS

CHAPTER FIVE
Print Advertising

Ever since Volney Palmer opened the world's first advertising agency in 1843, marketing professionals have been trying to answer the question, "What makes a good advertisement?" That this debate has never been settled is obvious to anyone who has ever created an ad for a client's approval—or tried to get a piece of copy approved.

Advertising results can be measured in several ways, including inquiries, focus groups, and readership studies. Yet a definitive measurement of the effectiveness of ads (other than direct response) remains elusive. Ad copy is evaluated on subjective criteria more frequently than by any other method. The reviewer either likes it, hates it, or is indifferent. And no two reviewers seem to agree on what makes for a good ad or a bad ad.

Despite the billions of dollars spent by American business in creating and running advertising, and testing and measuring advertising effectiveness, no one has discovered a magic formula that will ensure a winner every time. Even mail order advertisers, who can measure sales generated by their ads down to the penny, cannot guarantee or predict which ads will increase their client's profits and which won't.

At the same time we see that certain companies and ad agencies hit the mark more often than they miss while others don't. In this chapter we will explore the principles and methods that can help improve the odds that the next ad you create will be a winner—one that generates the immediate sales results you desire.

1. Advertise the right product for the right audience.

The first step is to make sure you are advertising a product that is potentially useful to the people you have targeted. This seems to be a simple and obvious rule. Yet, many clients believe that a great ad can sell anything to anyone. They are wrong.

"Copy cannot create desire for a product," writes Eugene Schwartz in his book *Breakthrough Advertising*. "It can only focus already-existing desires onto a particular product. The copywriter's task is not to create this mass desire, but to channel and direct it."

For example, no advertisement, no matter how powerfully written, will convince vegetarians to have a steak dinner at your new restaurant. But your ad might—if persuasively worded—entice them try your salad bar.

Charles Inlander, of the People's Medical Society, is a master at finding the right product for the right audience. His ad "Do you recognize the seven early warning signs of high blood pressure?" sold more than 20,000 copies of a $4.95 book on blood pressure when it ran ten times in *Prevention Magazine* over a three-year period.

"First, you select your topic," says Inlander, explaining the secret of his advertising success, "then you must find the right place to advertise. It's important to pinpoint a magazine whose readers are the right prospects for what you are selling." In other words, the right product for the right audience.

It's important to determine the readership of any publication you're thinking of advertising in. If you advertise in publications in which only a small percentage of the readers are prospects, you will be paying to reach too many people who are not potential buyers, and the ad will not pay off. The more targeted the publication is to your audience, the better your chances for success.

Who are your prospects? PC users? Runners? Gardeners? Mothers? Does your product satisfy a need or solve a problem for them? If not, you will have a difficult time. The right product for the audience will sell even if the ad is mediocre. The wrong product will not sell even if the ad is dynamite.

Look carefully at the publications in which you're thinking of running an ad. If there are ads for products similar to yours and these ads have been run repeatedly, that's a good sign: The publication must be working, or these advertisers would not be spending their money to run the ads over and over again.

If a publication does not contain ads for products similar to yours, you should hesitate to advertise there, even if the publication seems to reach the right audience. The lack of similar advertising is a good indicator that other advertisers may have tried the publication and found it wanting. Proceed with caution.

2. Use an attention-getting headline.

Next to the selection of subject matter and the placement of your ad in the proper publication, the headline is the most important element of your ad.

People flip through magazines and newspapers quickly. You have only a second or two to get them to stop and notice your ad. The headline plays a major role in doing this, as does the visual if there is one.

The main purpose of the headline is to grab the reader's attention and make her stop long enough to start reading your ad. You can achieve this in several ways. For example, here's an attention-grabbing headline from a newspaper ad:

IMPORTANT NEWS FOR WOMEN WITH FLAT OR THINNING HAIR

This headline is effective in gaining the attention of the potential client for two reasons: It promises important news, and it identifies the prospect for the service. Incidentally, this ad persuaded more than 1,200 readers a month to clip a coupon and send for a free brochure on a hair-conditioning procedure.

To promote a home-study course in writing for children, the Children's Institute of Literature has been using the same successful ad for decades. The headline reads:

WE'RE LOOKING FOR PEOPLE TO WRITE CHILDREN'S BOOKS

This headline works for several reasons. Like the thinning hair headline, it identifies the prospect for the service: people who want to write children's books. More importantly, it delays any reference to the fact that the ad is selling a home-study course, giving the reader sufficient time to get interested and involved before going into the offer. In fact, although the headline is completely honest, you get the impression initially that the ad is from a children's book publisher looking for authors, which grabs the attention of the would-be authors who are prospects for this course.

3. The lead paragraph should expand on the theme of the headline.

The lead must rapidly follow up on the idea expressed in the headline. If the headline asks a question, the lead should immediately answer it. The promises made to the reader in the headline (e.g., "Learn the secret to richer, moister chocolate cake") must be fulfilled in the first few paragraphs of copy. Otherwise, the reader feels disappointed and turns the page.

Here is an example of a well-written lead paragraph from an ad selling a business opportunity:

> QUIT YOUR JOB OR START PART-TIME
>
> *Chimney Sweeps Are Urgently Needed Now*
>
> My name is Tom Risch. I'm going to show you how to make $200 a day saving people from dangerous chimney fires....

Do not waste the reader's time with a "warm-up" paragraph. Instead, go straight to the heart of the matter. In editing a first draft, ask yourself, "Can I eliminate my first paragraph and start with my second or third paragraph?" Eight times out of ten, you can—and the copy will be stronger as a result.

4. Use a layout that draws the reader into the ad.

Take a look at some print ads right now. See if you can find any that draw your eye to the page and make reading a pleasure. This is the type of layout you want to use in your own ads. Avoid layouts that make the ad hard to read or discourage readers from even trying.

Your layout should have a focal point—a central, dominant visual element that draws the reader's eye to the page. This is usually the headline or the visual. But it might also be the coupon, or perhaps the lead paragraph of copy. When there are two or more equally prominent visuals competing for the eye's attention, readers become confused and don't know where to start reading. Always make one element larger and more prominent than the others.

Have the body copy set in serif type. Serif type has lines (serifs) at the end of the letter stems, as in this book. It is easier to read than sans serif, which has no such lines. Headlines can be set in either typeface.

Do not set large portions of the ad in reverse type (white on black). Avoid setting type against an illustration, photograph, or colored background. Use black type on a plain white background. It is easiest to read.

5. Write body copy supporting the idea presented in the opening.

What facts should be included in your body copy? Which should be left out? The decision is made by listing all the key points and then deciding which are the strongest and will best convince the reader to respond to your advertisement.

Start by listing all the features of the product and the benefits people can get from each feature. For instance, a *feature* of an air conditioner could be that its energy efficiency rating is 9.2; the *benefit* would then be a lower electric bill.

After making a complete list of features and benefits, list them in order of importance. Then begin your body copy with the most important benefit. Incorporate the rest of the benefits on your list. Now you've written copy that highlights the most important reasons to buy the product.

But display ads for publications have limited space. You don't have the freedom to go on at length as you do in a brochure or direct-mail package, so editing is an especially important part of writing good ads.

Here's one way to do it: First write the ad copy without regard to length. Get all your sales arguments in. Make the message complete. Then go back. Prune and edit, trimming the copy until it fits. This can be difficult. It's easy to "fall in love" with your copy and not want to cut any part of it. But you don't want to force the reader to use a magnifying glass to read your ad. The type size should be equal to or larger than the type size of the body type in the publication's articles.

See Chapter 3 for additional guidelines on writing effective body copy.

6. Be specific.

"Platitudes and generalities roll off the human understanding like water from a duck," wrote Claude Hopkins in his classic book, *Scientific Advertising.* "They leave no impression whatever."

The most common mistake we see in advertising today is "lazy copy"—copy written by copywriters who were too lazy to take the time to learn about their audience and understand the features and benefits of their product, the reasons why someone would want to buy it.

Why is so much ad copy vague and general? Two reasons.

First, it takes effort to research and understand a product and its market. It's difficult work, and ads are usually written on tight deadlines. Either there isn't time to gather facts or, more likely, writers take the easy route and write copy based only on the material at hand.

Second, some ad writers are not research-oriented. Some do not believe specifics are important. Many feel tone and emotion are all-important and that consumers do not want product facts. Experience shows that, for the most part, they are wrong.

Good advertising is effective largely because it is specific. There are two benefits to being specific. One, it gives customers the information they need to make a buying decision. Two, it creates believability. As Hopkins points out, people are more likely to believe a specific, factual claim than a boast, superlative, or generalization.

Does this mean that ad copy should be a litany of facts and figures? No. But the copywriter's best weapon is the selective use of facts to support the sales pitch. Here are some examples of well-written, specific, factual copy, taken from real ads:

> One out of every four Americans has high blood pressure. Yet only half these people know it. You may be one of them. If you are over forty, you owe it to yourself to have your blood pressure checked....

> The Mobilaire (R) 5000. 59 pounds of Westinghouse air conditioning in a compact unit that cools rooms 12' x 16' or smaller. Carry one home, install it in minutes—it plugs in like a lamp into any adequately wired circuit. Fits any window 19 1/8" to 42" wide.

> BluBlockers filter out blue light, making everything appear sharper, clearer and with a greater 3-dimensional look to it. Blue is the shortest light wave in the visible spectrum and focuses slightly in front of our retina which is the focusing screen in our eyes. By filtering out the blue in the BluBlocker

lenses, our vision is enhanced and everything appears to have a 3-dimensional look to it. But there's more....

Direct Marketing magazine reports on an experiment in which more than 70 retailers tested different ads and measured results. Here's what they found: When advertisers doubled the number of product facts in the ad, sales increased approximately 50 percent.

7. Focus on the prospect, not the product.

Of course, your ad must contain information about the product. But the information must be important to your prospects. It must be information they will find interesting or fascinating; information that will answer their questions, satisfy their curiosity, or cause them to believe the claims you make; information, in short, that will convince them to buy your product.

The reader's own concerns, needs, desires, fears, and problems are more important than your product, your company, and your goals. As copywriting expert Dr. Jeffrey Lant points out, good advertising copy is "client-centered." It focuses on the prospect and how your product solves his or her problems.

For instance, instead of saying, "We have more than 50 service centers nationwide," translate this statement into a reader benefit: "You'll be assured of prompt, courteous service and fast delivery of replacement parts from one of our 50 service centers located nationwide." Don't say "energy efficient" when you can say "cuts your electric bills in half."

The real star of your ad is the reader. Your product is secondary, and is of concern only in that it relates to a need, desire, or problem the reader has or a benefit he wants. Your company is the least important element of your copy, included only to reassure prospects that you are a reputable company that is financially stable.

Here are excerpts from ads that start with the prospects and their needs and concerns:

> Whether you love computers or hate them, there's no avoiding it:

> Today, computers are an essential tool for chemical engineers. To remain productive, you've got to keep up with the latest software and computing techniques.

But being a computer expert can be a full-time job.

The solution? You can go back to school and get a degree in computer science. Or, attend Chemputers '98.

———

Every day, law firms struggle with the expense and inconvenience of engraved and preprinted stationery.

Now you can select the best mutual funds for any portfolio...<u>faster and easier than ever</u>... to become a <u>hero</u> with your clients. And ensure that they invest their money with you, again and again.

———

Need extrusion wear parts that last longer? Ferro-Tic HT-6A is the answer.

———

Are you sick and tired of your current job?

Do you dream of a career that's fun, exciting—and financially rewarding?

Do you enjoy going on vacation, traveling to exotic locations, and seeing the world?

If so, the Echols International Tourism Institute has some exciting news for you about career opportunities in today's travel industry.

8. Write in a clear, simple, conversational style.

According to *Business Marketing* magazine's Copy Chasers, a panel of judges who regularly critique advertising in a monthly column, good ad copy should sound like "one friend talking to another."

We agree. Copy should not be pompous, remote, aloof, or written in "corporatese." The most effective copy is written in a plain, simple, conversational style—the way a sincere person talks when she wants to help or advise you.

Madison Avenue has created an accepted style for ad copy that some of the big agencies now use. This "style" is the type of copy that seems to deliberately remind you that you are reading an ad. It is self-conscious copy. Avoid this type of slick lingo.

Read the sample copy scattered throughout this book. This is the style and tone you want to achieve. Also see chapter 3 for a more in-depth discussion of how to write clear, concise body copy.

A deliberate attempt to achieve a certain style in copy usually has the effect of calling attention to the writing itself and diverting consumers away from the message. It makes readers aware they are "reading an ad." The focus should be on the prospect and the product, not the ad or the copywriter.

Here are some examples, taken from recent print ads, of copy that achieves the natural, easy-flowing tone you want in your ads. Even ads for technical products should sound friendly, inviting, and understandable:

> The travel business is the world's fastest growing industry. Trained personnel are desperately needed by hotels...airlines...tour companies...cruise lines...convention centers...and travel agencies—both here and abroad. Now Echols can give you the training to help you qualify.

> Making dies, guides, die rings, die holders, mandrels, baskets, and fixtures from HT-6A enables your wear parts to work through millions of cycles. Dies last longer, reducing downtime and replacement costs in hot and cold extrusion processes.

> You may have read that *today* the lending climate is friendlier. Don't believe it! The fact is, only *larger* corporations have ready access to capital. Growing businesses looking for funding are often up against a brick wall.

> Chemputers is the only computer users conference specifically designed for chemical engineers. In just 48 hours, you'll learn things about computers—and chemical engineering—

that your colleagues won't get in an entire year of reading journals and going to trade shows.

Your style may be slightly different. That's fine. But we have found that "reader-friendly" ads have several things in common: simple language, short sentences, and short paragraphs. Copy should address the reader directly; the word *you* should appear frequently.

Use informal language, contractions, sentence fragments, and conversational tone—even a slang phrase now and then. A good ad sounds like one person talking to another about a subject of mutual interest.

9. Ask for a response—and make it easy to reply.

There are three easy steps for turning your ad into a response-generating marketing tool.

Decide what type of response you want. What action do you want the reader to take? Do you want your prospect to phone or write you, or clip a coupon and mail it back to you? Do you want the reader to visit your store, request a copy of your catalog or sales brochure, set up an appointment to see a salesperson, test-drive your product, or order your product directly from the ad? Decide what you want the reader to do.

Tell the reader to do it. The last few paragraphs of your copy should spell out the action you want the reader to take and give him reasons to take it. For instance:

> Just clip the coupon or call toll-free now and we'll send you the next issue FREE without obligation as a special introduction to *Employment Guide.*

> So why not call 1-800-FIND4WD for a dealer convenient to you?

> Just send in the card (or the coupon) and have some fun with your first issue. Then pay us *after* you've taken a look.

And send for Display Masters' invaluable FREE booklet on point-of-purchase marketing, "33 Ways to Better Displays: What Every Marketing Executive Should Know About Point-of-Purchase Displays in Today's Market."

Give the reader a reason to respond. These reasons can include any of the following:

- Free booklet or catalog
- Free brochure
- Bonus gift
- Price list or cost estimate
- Discount or sale
- Time-limited offer
- Free initial consultation or evaluation

Give the reader a mechanism for responding. Emphasize this mechanism in your ad layout to simplify the process of making contact with you.

In print advertising, this is accomplished through the use of a toll-free phone number (usually printed in large type to attract attention to it) or by including a coupon in the ad.

Some magazines also allow you to insert a reply card, which is bound into the magazine and appears opposite your ad. This is an expensive technique, but it can dramatically increase replies.

Make it easy for your reader to get in touch should he want to do business with you. This means always including an address and telephone number (preferably toll-free), fax number, and e-mail and Web site addresses.

CHAPTER SIX
Direct Mail

D irect mail holds particular fascination for many marketers because it is one of the few promotional methods whose results can be measured directly and precisely. Here are 20 copywriting techniques that can make your direct-mail package lively, engaging, compelling, and much more effective in generating leads and sales.

1. Empathize with the reader.

Direct-mail professionals use the term *affinity group* to describe a market segment of people with similar interests. Stamp collectors, freelance writers, automobile enthusiasts, pet owners, IBM PC users, bodybuilders, and joggers are all examples of affinity groups.

Members of affinity groups often have strong feelings about their particular interest. Perhaps you have a friend who talks endlessly about bits, bytes, and other computer jargon. It may bore you silly, but to him it's sheer joy. Do you have a special hobby or interest? Then you know how much fun it is to share it with other people.

When writing to affinity groups, demonstrate that you are in sync with them and that you are as knowledgeable and enthusiastic as they are. Here's an example of "empathy" copy from a letter offering a subscription to *Practical Homeowner* magazine:

> Dear Homeowner,
>
> Do you enjoy your home? I mean really enjoy it? Does it still feel good at the end of the day to walk through that door, kick off your shoes, and just be...home?

By showing the reader that you are "simpatico" with his needs, you are already halfway to winning him over as a friend—and a customer.

2. Use the "Ah-Ha" factor.

One way to get prospects on your side is to tell them something they already know.

The trick is not to tell them something mundane or blatantly obvious, but to bring to the surface a fact, perception, or emotion the reader may not have been aware of—and thereby evoke a reaction of "ah-ha" or "yes, of course" or "that's right!"

The power of this technique is that we all like to learn more about ourselves and our state of mind. The ah-ha technique builds your credibility by reinforcing and dramatizing the reader's own knowledge or beliefs.

Here's an example from a letter selling a home-study program on money management and investing:

> Dear Reader:
>
> My name is Morton Shulman. I am a medical doctor by training, and I still maintain an active practice. I make a good living as a doctor, but I realized long ago that you can't get rich on a salary alone, not even a doctor's salary. So I turned to investing.

Most of us rely on our salaries, not investments, for income. We know deep down that we can't get rich this way, but through laziness, lack of time, or lack of knowledge, we don't do much about it. That's why Dr. Shulman's letter really hits home. When we read it, we say, "Yes, he's right; we ought to be smarter about handling our money"— which is the exact frame of mind a company selling an investment program wants to create.

3. Turn a potential negative into a positive.

In his classic book *Tested Advertising Methods,* John Caples quotes the following story by Jim Young, who ran a mail-order apple business:

> *A few years ago there was a hail storm just before harvest. I had thousands of mail orders and checks, and almost every*

apple was hail-pocked. Problem: Should I send the checks back or risk dissatisfied customers? Actually these apples were damaged only in appearance. They were better eating than ever. Cold weather, when apples are ripening, improves their flavor. So I filled the orders. In every carton I put a printed card:

"Note the hail marks which have caused minor skin blemishes on some of these apples. These are proof of their growth at a high mountain altitude, where the sudden chills from hail storms help firm the flesh and develop the natural fruit sugars which give these apples their incomparable flavor."

Not one customer complained. Next year I received orders which said: "Hail marked apples, if available; otherwise the ordinary kind."

Another example of turning a negative into a positive is the Harry and David mail-order catalog advertising their famous Royal Riviera Pears. The copy says of the pears, "So unusual that not one person in a thousand has ever tasted them," which of course make them seem even more desirable. But if you stop and think about it, you realize this well-turned phrase also says, "Not too many people buy this product"…which, if presented in those terms, might have a negative effect on sales.

4. Ask a provocative question.
"Do you want me to give you a surefire way of improving direct-mail response?" That's an example of a question used to grab the reader's attention and heighten his interest.

Question leads can be extremely effective if the lead (a) arouses the reader's curiosity, or (b) deals with a timely, important, or controversial issue, or (c) asks a question the buyer genuinely wants the answer to. Some examples:

What Do Japanese Managers Have That American Managers Sometimes Lack? (The Economics Press)

If You Were To Find Out Today That You Had Only A Short Time To Live, Would You Feel Comfortable With The Amount Of Life Insurance That You Have Provided Your Family? (United Of Omaha)

Is There A Roll Of Film In Your Camera Right Now? (Kodak)

5. Make a quick transition from your opening to the sales pitch.

Don't waste time with warm-up paragraphs. After grabbing the reader's attention, quickly shift the focus and begin making your sales pitch. People are busy and appreciate letters that get to the point. In a fund-raising letter, the American Red Cross makes a fast transition from the reader's concerns to the Red Cross's plight in only two paragraphs:

Dear Friend:

When disaster strikes your home you may urgently need the Red Cross.

But right now during the holiday season the Red Cross urgently needs you....

6. Use details.

Be specific. It's not enough to claim that a product is better, faster, easier, or cheaper when you can state the specific figures and facts. Adding them makes your copy interesting and believable. As copywriter Don Hauptman puts it: "Superlatives are often not credible; concretes invariably have the ring of truth." Some examples:

The nationwide leader in dental-practice collections, IC Systems has collected past-due accounts receivables for 45,717 dental practices since 1963. Over 20 state dental associations recommend our services to their members.

<u>We guarantee the best technical service and support.</u> I was a compressor service technician at Ingersoll Rand, and in the last 20 years have personally serviced more than 250 compressors at over 80 companies.

―――――――

Importantly, even if you are already taking calcium, you may still need to take calcium AEP. That's because the 2-amino ethanol phosphate—not calcium—is the active MS-fighting ingredient. The 2-amino ethanol phosphate protects the integrity of cell membranes, sealing them off from autoimmune complexes but permitting nutrients to enter. This makes calcium AEP effective in treating not only MS but a wide range of other autoimmune diseases—including arthritis and lupus.

7. Be sincere.

In a recent survey the Simmons Market Research Bureau asked people what they disliked most about direct marketing. Forty-one percent said "deception." But contrary to the image the general public might have of direct marketing techniques, the majority of direct marketing professionals are honest and strive to tell the truth in their mailings.

This isn't entirely altruistic, of course. Through experience, direct marketers have learned that while they might be able to trick customers with deceptive advertising once, a buyer who feels duped will not buy a second time. And repeat sales represent the bulk of profits in most business enterprises. So it is more profitable to be honest than to be deceptive or misleading or to tell outright lies.

People are turned off by direct mail that seems insincere, too high pressure, or dishonest. But how can you sound sincere in your letters? By *being* sincere! If what you're saying isn't true, it will come through in the copy.

Ask other people to read your letters and tell you whether your copy rings true. In their zeal to sell products, copywriters sometimes overstate their cases, damaging credibility.

Woodbridge Memorial Gardens sent a letter that failed to convince us of their concern for our well-being. It begins:

Dear Neighbor:

It is very disturbing to me to think that you may lose the last opportunity to own your personal, aboveground mausoleum at a price that can save you so much money and heartache.

Maybe we're cynics, but we would have found the letter more credible if the writer said he was "concerned." "Disturbed" seemed to be overstating the case.

Another letter that failed to motivate us was this fund-raising solicitation from the American Kidney Fund.

Dear Friend:

I wouldn't write you like this if it weren't truly urgent.

Our reaction? "Of course you would. It's your job to raise funds. What else would you be doing with your time aside from writing to people like us?"

8. Avoid contradictions.

When reviewing your copy, be sure to check for consistency and eliminate contradictions between statements. When people read contradictory statements in your mailings, it destroys your credibility. Their reaction is: "These people don't know what they're talking about!"

A factual error is much worse than any grammatical error or typo you can make. In a letter offering a set of gourmet recipe cards, the writer contradicts herself in the first sentence:

Dear Gourmet,

You may never again have to worry about time for cooking....

See the contradiction? Gourmets don't worry about cooking; they enjoy it! They may worry about housework or gardening or shopping. But they'll always make time to prepare a good meal.

9. Narrow the focus.

The narrower your audience, the more specific you can be about meeting their needs. When people see their specific requirements addressed in an ad or mailer, they are more likely to respond than if the ad is making a broad appeal to all readers.

The best way to do this is to target copy at specific market niches. For example, if you're a computer company specializing in systems for law offices, the headline "Computerize Your Law Practice for Under $6,500" is better than "Computerize Your Business!"

You can talk to your audience in terms of their specific job title, profession, industry, lifestyle, income level, or whatever else is appropriate. The headline "Important Life Insurance News for Men and Women Over 59" will attract more prospects age 59 and over than the headline "Important Life Insurance News!"

10. Make your product sound irresistible.

The master of this technique is the copywriter for Harry and David's Fruit of the Month Club:

> Few things are finer on a summer's eve than a slice of this buttery loaf cake, heaped with fresh, naturally sweet Oregold slices. Top with whipped cream, or a little raspberry syrup, makes a deliciously different gift... .

> Velvety black, one to a mouthful Belgian hothouse type, these luscious grapes were once reserved exclusively for European royalty.

> Huge, luscious peaches grown right here in the Rogue River Valley, where rich volcanic soil, crisp cool nights and pure mountain water nurture these beauties to juicy, plump perfection. Shipped so fresh you can almost smell the orchards in bloom!

11. Use fear as a motivator.

Fear is one of the most powerful human motivators. Fear sells us on many things, including alarm systems, life insurance, home medical tests, and childproof medicine bottles. Use it to your advantage when appropriate.

A recent mailing from American Family Publishers included a letter from (who else?) Ed McMahon. While the central theme of the promotion was, "Enter the contest and win $10 million," Ed's letter approached it from a different angle: namely, if you don't enter, you could be losing $10 million.

> If you return the winning number in time, I'll be personally handing you the first ten million dollars. But, if you decide to ignore this letter and throw your exclusive numbers away, I'll surely be awarding all the money to someone else.
>
> PREVIOUS WINNERS HAVE THROWN THEIR NUMBERS RIGHT INTO THE TRASH—THEY LITERALLY THREW AWAY MILLIONS!

This approach can be very effective. We've all heard that little nagging voice that tells us not to throw away a sweepstakes mailing because we could be throwing away a chance at a million dollars. But, because we're busy, we trash it anyway. This letter plays on that fear, hoping to persuade us to enter the drawing.

12. Anticipate the prospect's most likely complaint.

If you can address your prospect's biggest complaint about, objection to, or problem with your product or service, and tackle it in your letter, you'll have hooked the reader into your sales pitch and created a lot of goodwill in the process.

Here's a fund-raising letter from Channel Thirteen, a local public television station in New York, that comes to grips with a pet peeve of many viewers:

> For years, people like you have commented....
>
> "I'll tell you why I don't give to THIRTEEN. It's those pledge drives! If you would just take those drives off the air and give me the intelligent TV I love, then I'd become a member!"
>
> Well, last year we took you up on this challenge by canceling two of our three life-sustaining pledge drives. And, we're going to take this huge gamble again.

The message here is: "Hey, we listened to your complaints and we did what you asked. Now how about helping us out in return?"

13. Make your offer in the first few paragraphs.

If you suspect that people are not likely to read your letter, you can boost the number of responses by making your offer right up front. This way, the reader who only glances at the opening of your letter still gets the gist of your message and learns about your offer.

Here's the opening of a letter promoting life insurance policies for children. A free booklet containing details of the insurance is offered right up front.

There's no gift more meaningful...

...for the children you love than the one discussed in a new free pamphlet. It is yours with my compliments if you'll just mail the card enclosed.

14. Flatter the reader.

As long as you don't overdo it, flattery *will* get you everywhere. Or almost everywhere. The American Museum of Natural History portrays the recipients of this letter as perhaps more noble and good than they really are:

Dear Reader:

From all indications available to us, you're a rather uncommon person.

One who has a special reverence for our natural surroundings...an endless and respectful curiosity about the quirks of animal and human nature...an unabashed sense of wonder and fascination in the presence of our legacy from the past.

15. Inject a personal note into the copy.

In some situations a "human touch" can add drama and impact to your mailing piece. For example, if your business is giving seminars on public speaking and you once had a humiliating experience while giving a presentation, this can form the basis of a very personal letter in which you empathize with similar experiences the prospect may have had.

Here's the opening of a hard-hitting fund-raising appeal:

> Dear Ms. Smith:
>
> Do you remember me? I am Don McNeill, and I was privileged to come into the homes of millions of Americans like you during the more than 30 years that I hosted *The Breakfast Club* on ABC radio.
>
> I am now involved in one of the most important battles of my life: the battle to find a cure for Alzheimer's Disease.
>
> This cruel disease killed my wife, Kay. My concern now is for the 120,000 people who will die of Alzheimer's Disease this year, next year, and each year thereafter....

Obviously the personal nature of this note strikes a chord. Who cannot help but feel sympathy for the writer and empathy for his cause?

16. Highlight your guarantee.

A strong guarantee is reassuring to people who haven't done business with you before. So emphasize your guarantee in your copy.

A self-mailer from Atlantic Fasteners shows a picture of company president Patrick J. O'Toole holding up a certificate good for a $50 credit on the purchase of any fasteners sold by his firm. The headline and subhead underneath the photo read:

> YOU GET NEXT-DAY DELIVERY FROM OUR STOCK OF 28,981,000 FASTENERS, OR I SEND YOU A $50 CREDIT! Only two credits issued in last 9,322 orders.

Make your guarantee generous, long-term, and unconditional. A 30-day money-back guarantee will usually pull more orders than a 10-day money-back guarantee. A 60- or 90-day guarantee is even better.

Don't worry that by stressing your guarantee, you'll get more people taking advantage of it. The experience of hundreds of mail order companies indicates that people are basically honest. Only an insignificant percentage will try to dupe you.

17. Make it easy to respond.

The easier you make it to reply to your mailing, the more replies you'll get.

How do you simplify the response process?

- Give people the option of calling for more information or sending back a business reply card.

- Include your fax number and e-mail address.

- Use a loose reply card or order form rather than a reply element that has to be separated from a letter or brochure.

- Don't ask a lot of questions in your reply element. Just get the minimum amount of information you need to fulfill the reader's order or request.

- Leave plenty of room for the reader to fill in the required information.

- Use business reply mail that does not require the reader to supply a stamp.

- When seeking orders, provide a toll-free number and accept major credit cards. According to InfoMat Marketing, a California-based ad agency specializing in direct response, an "800" number and a credit card payment option can increase your response by as much as 30 percent.

- When seeking inquiries or orders from business customers, include your fax number and encourage the recipient to fax the completed order form to you. Make sure the reply form is on white paper or other light-colored stock to ensure readability when it is faxed.

18. Use the two most powerful words in direct-mail copywriting: *You* and *Free.*

Your copy should address the reader directly, as a person. Use the word *you* in your copy. When you review your copy, make sure you have used *you* frequently. A lot of *you*'s indicates that you are speaking directly to the reader.

"This magic word—'you'—makes direct mail personal," writes Robert Stuber in *U.S.A. Directions* (Vol. 4, No. 3, page 3). "It raises the letter—even one that has thousands in circulation—to a very personal level. It flatters the reader and builds a relationship."

On the other hand, if you see *I*, or *we*, or *our company* too often, you know your copy is too advertiser-oriented.

Here's a piece of copy that does a good job of speaking directly to the reader:

> YOU ASKED FOR THE FULL STORY OF THE SANDIER SELLING SYSTEM
>
> …and here it is. But the real story is about you. About how you can take a giant step up, right now. A step up in the number of sales you close…the quality of those sales…the money you make. And just as important, an enormous gain in satisfaction and professional pride.

Don't forget the other magic word of direct mail copywriting: *Free.*

People love to get free things. If you are generating leads and offering a brochure or catalog, say that it is free. If you are selling a product and offering a premium, stress the free gift. If you offer a money-back guarantee, say the customer can examine your product on a risk-free trial basis. "The word 'free' simply can't be beat," says Stuber. "Generally, the more it is used, the better."

Even a simple teaser such as "Special FREE offer inside" can get people who would otherwise not be tempted by your offer to open the envelope.

19. Demonstrate your product.

If there is any way you can economically demonstrate your product in your mailing, do it. Few things are as convincing as an actual demonstration.

An innovative industrial promotion advertised a chemical used in fireproofing. The headline of the ad challenged the reader: "Try Burning This Coupon." A match set the page ablaze, but when you removed the match, the fire went out! The copy explained that the page (produced by the manufacturer and bound as an insert into the magazine) was treated with the fire-retardant compound being advertised. A brilliant example of a demonstration in print.

How do you demonstrate your product in direct mail? Remember, a mailing can consist of more than a letter and brochure. You can include a product sample, a demo diskette, a test kit, a material swatch. There are many opportunities to let the customer try your product before ordering.

Seton Name Plate sends a sample Property Identification Plate along with the following letter of instruction:

> Try this simple test. With a ballpoint pen, write your initials next to the numbers on the enclosed sample plate. Now try to erase both. Let me save you the trouble…you can't erase them without defacing the tag.

Potential customers don't have to take Seton's word that the plates are permanent. They can see it for themselves. Believability is increased perhaps a hundredfold.

20. Promise to share a secret.

Exclusivity is another powerful direct-mail motivator. People like to feel that they are getting inside information, or becoming the first on their block to get something new, or getting in on the ground floor of a good deal.

Boardroom Classics, a book publisher, uses a six-page letter to sell its $29.95 *Book of Inside Information*. The opening lines of the letter read:

> WHAT CREDIT CARD COMPANIES DON'T TELL YOU. PAGE 10.
>
> What hospitals don't tell you. Page 421.
>
> What the IRS doesn't tell you. Page 115.
>
> What the airlines don't tell you. Page 367.
>
> What car dealers don't tell you….

We know this letter is successful because Boardroom mails it five times or more within a 12-month period. They would not repeat it so frequently unless it was profitable. As a rule, repeat mailings are a good indicator of what is working for other advertisers in direct mail. And Boardroom enjoys a reputation as one of the most successful direct marketers of books, newsletters, and other "information products."

CHAPTER SEVEN

Brochures

While many businesses can't afford print advertising or TV commercials, nearly every organization has a brochure of some kind. This chapter presents ten guidelines to help you write more effective copy for brochures of all types.

1. Start selling on the cover.

Whether someone receives your literature in the mail or plucks it off a rack, it is the cover that makes your prospect either read further, set it aside, or throw it out. Yet the majority of advertisers waste the front cover. They decorate it with the product name, a fancy graphic, or the company logo, and hope that will be sufficient to prod the reader to go on. It's not.

The cover should display a strong selling message, ideally in headline form. This message can identify the audience for the product or service, stress the usefulness of the product, or highlight other potential benefits.

A well thought-out cover headline increases the selling power of the piece. Take, for example, the headline and opening lines on a pamphlet promoting a bank's Christmas club:

IMAGINE HAVING AN EXTRA $520 FOR THE HOLIDAYS

It's easy.

It's painless.

It's automatic.

It's just $10 a week.

The headline here is more likely to grab a depositor's attention than a pamphlet labeled, "Christmas Club Account."

Here are some other effective headlines taken from actual brochures:

> IBM proudly announces <u>affordable</u> desktop ATM:
>
> ATM 25 Mbps Workgroup Solutions—now only $495 per user!
>
> *Now there's an easy way to implement interactive multimedia in your broadband network products*
>
> Boosting melting productivity and efficiency with oxy-fuel combustion
>
> Seamlessly integrating telephony and computer technology

A headline isn't the only way to begin selling on the cover. Telling a story illustrated with one or more dramatic photographs is another option. A booklet used in a fund-raising mailing for an animal welfare society might feature heartbreaking photos of mistreated animals. Usually, though, words and pictures together are stronger than images alone.

2. Make your story flow.

A brochure is in many ways like a miniature book, and like a good book, a good brochure tells a story. That story should have a beginning, a middle, and an ending, and flow smoothly from one point to the next.

Once you've written the first draft, sit back and read it as you would an article or short story. Does it progress logically? Or are there points where the transitions are awkward, where you are jarred by a phrase or sentence that doesn't seem to belong?

If the transitions aren't smooth, perhaps the material needs a bit of editing. Maybe adding a heading or a sentence or two will take care of the problem. Or perhaps a transitional phrase can bridge the gap between one sentence and the next. Here are some of the transitional words and phrases that copywriters use to make a sensible connection between copy points:

Additionally,	For example,	Plus,
Also,	For instance,	The reason:
And	Here's how:	The results?
Another reason is	Here's why:	Remember:
As a result,	However,	Similarly,
as well as	If…, then	Since
As we've discussed,	Imagine:	Still,
At the same time,	In addition,	That's where…can help
Best of all,	In other words,	Then again,
But	In this way,	Therefore,
But wait. There's more:	Moreover,	There's more:
By comparison,	Most important,	Thus,
Chances are	Obviously,	To be sure,
Even better,	Of course,	What's more,
Even worse,	On the other hand,	Why? Because…
First,… Second,… Third,…	Or	Yet,
	Perhaps	

3. Strive for a personal tone.

Write your brochure copy in a natural, relaxed, friendly style. Strive for the easy, conversational tone of spoken language—the short words, the short sentences, the personal touch. If what you've written sounds stiff, unnatural, or dull, it's not conversational and you need to revise it. Your copy should make people want to do business with your organization.

Some examples from recent brochures:

> Today we live in the Age of Now…the nanosecond 90s. When customers order a product, they want it right away.

You must deliver—fast. Or your customer might find someone else who can.

An oxygen supplier who knows only oxygen is of limited
value. But an oxygen supplier who knows oxygen *and* EAF
steelmaking—like BOC Gases—can be the strategic part-
ner who gives you a sustainable competitive advantage in
today's metals marketplace.

Losing your hair. It happens to millions of men. Yet unlike
the millions of men who are actually walking around with
bald heads, *you* have the power to do something about it.
Now. Before it's too late.

4. Stress benefits, not features.

Too many promotional brochures stress the *features* of the product or
service—the bare facts about how it works, what it looks like, how it is
made, where it is made, who designed it, and so on.

Effective copy translates features into benefits—what the product
can do for customers. Benefits are the reasons why customers should
buy the product.

After you identify the key features of your product, make a corre-
sponding list of benefits. Here is a partial list for a familiar item—
a clock radio:

Feature	Benefit
Large illuminated digital display	Time easy to see at a glance—even at night.
Snooze alarm switch	Tired? Just hit a button for 10 more minutes of sleep.
Digital alarm	Alarm wakes you at precisely the right time.
Wood veneer finish	Handsome design will complement your bedroom decor.

Feature	Benefit
Felt pads on bottom	Won't scratch or smudge furniture.
Alarm/radio option	Wake to the sound that suits you— gentle strings, hard rock, or the buzz of an alarm.
AM/FM	Get all your favorite stations.

5. Be specific.

People read brochures because they want information. And they are quickly turned off by brochures that are long on puffery and short on content.

So be specific. Don't write, "saves you money" when you can say "reduces fuel consumption up to 50 percent." Don't say "we're reliable" if you can tell the customer, "The repairman arrives within 24 hours or we fix it free of charge." Don't be content to talk about "a lot of energy saved" if you know your insulation "reduces heating bills by 30 to 50 percent a month." Remember, specifics sell.

6. Support your claims.

Even if you stress benefits instead of features, even if you make specific claims, the customer still may not believe you. In his book *Direct Mail Copy That Sells*, copywriter Herschell Gordon Lewis describes modern times as an Age of Skepticism:

> *This is the Age in which nobody believes anybody, in which claims of superiority are challenged just because they're claims, in which consumers express surprise when something they buy actually performs the way it was advertised to perform.*

How can you overcome skepticism and get people to believe you? Here are some things to include in your brochure:

- **Guarantees.** Offer a guarantee: money back, free replacement, unlimited service, work redone at no cost. Guarantees allow the customer to try the product at no risk and ensure satisfaction.

- **Testimonials.** A testimonial is a statement of praise or endorsement from a satisfied customer (or, in some cases, a celebrity). The testimonial is written in the customer's own words, appears in quotation marks, and is usually attributed to a specific person.

- **Case histories.** Case histories are product success stories. They tell how a particular customer benefited by selecting, buying, and using your product. They present the reasons why the customer selected your product over competitive items and the results achieved through its application.

- **Trials.** Let customers use your product with no risk or obligation to buy for a trial period.

- **Personal demonstrations.** Some products can be demonstrated only in person, either by a salesperson or a qualified technician. In that case you can state in your brochure copy that you can prove your claims with a live product demonstration in the customer's home or office or at your place. Then urge the prospect to contact you to arrange this demonstration.

- **Test results.** Has your product proven its superior performance in tests? If so, include the test results in your copy.

- **FAQs (Frequently Asked Questions).** If what you say in the copy is likely to raise questions in the consumer's mind, put the reader at ease by answering these questions in that same piece of copy.

- **Evidence of your reputation and stability.** Prove your reputation and stability by talking about your track record and past successes. Cite the number of years in the business, the size of your operation, number of employees, number of offices, number of warehouses, number of plants, annual sales, profits, and reputation.

- **Illustrations.** Help customers visualize how your product works or is put together and why this makes it better. For example, a flier claims a new four-step dental procedure to be quicker and easier than the conventional method. The flier shows a series of photos and captions to demonstrate the new procedure, step by step. You can use the same technique to demonstrate many products: a blender, a dishwasher, a lawn mower, a do-it-yourself home repair kit.

- **Comparisons.** If your product or service clearly beats the competition, you can include comparisons, as long as they can be supported by documentation (i.e., specifications taken from competitors' brochures).

Remember it's more effective to show than tell. Don't just say your product or service saves money or improves life. Show that it does. Say you're selling an energy-efficient air conditioner. Instead of just talking in a general sense about energy savings, provide sample calculations that show *exactly* how much money buyers can save based on their utility rates, room size, and the unit's BTU rating. Make it easy for the reader to follow the calculation and come up with money saved based on his specific situation.

7. Keep the copy lively.

Most copywriting texts tell you to keep sentences short, because short sentences are easier to read. But writing gets monotonous when all sentences are the same length. So vary sentence length. Every so often, put in a fairly long sentence. Also use an occasional very short sentence or sentence fragment. Like this one.

Lively writing is personal, not impersonal. Personal pronouns *(we, they, us, you)* make the copy sound less lawyerlike, more like person-to-person conversation. Addressing the reader directly as *you* in the copy adds warmth and creates the illusion in the reader's mind that the copy was specifically written just for her or him.

Human beings have been telling and recording stories since the first cave dwellers drew crude pictures of their hunting experiences on cave walls. Storytelling is an inherently powerful technique for getting your message across, much more so than a dry recitation of facts.

You can use storytelling to liven up your promotional copy. For example, instead of just stating that your bottle-coating process is superior, tell how one of your customers actually doubled his bottling business because of your better coating, got rich, and retired to Florida at age 51. People have a great interest in other people.

Separate and highlight key information. If you need to include product specifications, for example, put them in a separate table or sidebar, and keep your body copy lively. (A sidebar is a short article or section of copy separated from the main text and enclosed in a box or other graphic device.)

8. Make sure the information is relevant.

All copy should be interesting to read, but not everything that's interesting to read belongs in your copy.

Copy should be relevant both to the message you're trying to communicate and to the people you want to reach—those who are most likely to buy your product, join your club, take your course, or donate to your cause.

If a brochure selling industrial batteries begins with a two-page essay on the history of batteries, that may interest a science buff. But the industrial engineer looking for specific information on battery size and performance may not be willing to wade through this nonessential copy to get to the size, price, and performance data.

9. Check for accuracy.

Then check it again. Then have three or four other people in your organization check it, too. A single mistake can result in having to reprint the entire brochure. And that's expensive. So even though proofreading is boring, it's well worth the time and effort.

In addition to accuracy, you should also check for consistency. Make sure you've used the same style of grammar, punctuation, capitalization, spelling, numbers (figures vs. spelling out), abbreviations, titles, and product names throughout the copy. You're inconsistent if you write "GAF" in some places and "G.A.F." in others.

10. Don't forget the details.

One manufacturer spent $2,400 revising and reprinting its product sheets only to discover that the location of the company's new $20,000 Web site had been omitted on the new sheets!

We devote so much time and energy to the promotional aspect of our literature that we sometimes shortchange the details. But these details can be just as important as your sales pitch and graphic images.

Review your copy before it goes to the printer. Make sure you have included the following:

- Company name
- Logo
- Address
- Phone numbers and extensions, including toll-free numbers
- Hours to call
- Fax number
- E-mail address
- Web site address
- Store hours, locations, and directions
- Credit cards accepted
- Branch offices, including addresses and directions
- Telex and TWX
- Guarantee
- Disclaimers
- Other required legal wording
- Brochure date and code number
- Permissions and acknowledgments
- Trademarks and registration marks
- Copyright notice
- Product codes and other official emblems (e.g., Good House-keeping seal, Underwriters Laboratory).

The lack of this so-called fine print can kill the effectiveness of an otherwise fine promotion. For example, one restaurant handed out hundreds of promotional fliers offering a substantial savings on a fine dinner at their grand opening. The flier was widely distributed but brought in little business. Why? Because the restaurant was in a hard-to-find location, and although the flier contained the address, it didn't give directions, and potential customers couldn't find the place.

CHAPTER EIGHT
Catalogs

This chapter provides tips and techniques on writing more effective catalog copy.

While most ads and commercials feature a single product, catalogs offer multiple products. Some catalogs feature every product a company sells; others focus on a specific product line or a selection of products chosen according to a specific criterion, such as Christmas gift items.

Aside from the mailing list, the three most important elements of the catalog are its merchandising, graphics, and copy.

Merchandising refers to the selection of items for the catalog, their relative placement within the catalog, and the amount of space devoted to each item. Mail-order marketers use *square-inch analysis*— a tool that shows the amount of mail-order sales generated by each item in the catalog on the basis of dollars per space—to calculate how much space each item deserves. The most profitable items get more space and a more prominent position. The less profitable items get less space or may be dropped from the catalog altogether.

Graphics refers to the style of photographs and illustrations, layout of the pages, typography, colors, paper stock, and the quality of the printing. Almost every catalog relies, at least to some extent, on visual appeal to do a portion of the selling.

Copy refers to the text that accompanies the product photos and drawings. Depending on the product line, copy may be subordinate to visuals, play an equal role with visuals, or, more rarely, be more important than visuals.

While copy may not be the driving force in catalogs, it is one of the three key elements affecting a catalog's sales performance and should not be underestimated. The techniques outlined in this chapter can help you create copy that makes your catalog a more effective sales tool.

1. Match the length, format, and tone of your copy to the style of the catalog.

In catalogs, space is typically the primary limitation placed upon the copywriter. If you have only one column-inch per item, you've got to write lean, bare-bones, telegraphic copy. Write the basic facts, and nothing more.

On the other hand, if you have a full-page per item, you have the luxury of writing a conversational, ad-style sales pitch on each product. Keep in mind, however, that length alone does not make copy better. Rambling on and saying little is not writing good selling copy. But if your products can't be adequately described in the space available, you should consider adding more pages.

The copy style should be appropriate for the type of product being sold. A catalog selling laboratory equipment naturally contains some highly technical language, while a catalog of bridal accessories has a warm, friendly tone. The complexity of the product also affects the length of the copy; you can say more about a microprocessor than you can about a stick of chewing gum.

A catalog from which the customer can order directly must have complete product information and technical specifications. The description must give readers all the information they need to order the product. This includes sizes, styles, colors, materials, and prices. Copy has to be clear, comprehensive, and to the point.

A catalog used as a sales aid can contain more persuasive copy than the direct-order catalog. A promotional catalog designed to whet the customer's appetite will contain benefit-oriented headlines and subheads, highly sales-oriented body copy, and sophisticated graphics to engage the reader's attention. Remember, however, that no matter what the purpose of your catalog, not giving enough product details can be a sales deterrent. The promotional catalog lacking sufficient information will not stimulate the customer's interest enough to buy the product.

Length and content of copy depend not just on the product but also on the target audience. How sophisticated is the buyer? How much does he already know about the product and its uses? A paint catalog aimed at professional painters need only describe the color, composition, and other features of the various paints. A catalog selling paint to ordinary consumers would have to provide more of an education in the basics: types of paints available, benefits of each, and applications best suited to each kind of paint.

If your buyers are already sold on your firm and have a tradition of doing business with you, your catalog can contain simple, straightforward descriptions of your latest offerings. On the other hand, prospects who don't know you and your firm will have to be convinced that they should do their business with you instead of your competitors. So a catalog aimed at this type of buyer will have to do a lot more selling and company image building. The type of relationship you wish to have with your customers will also affect the tone you use (warm and friendly, formal and highly professional, etc.).

2. Use colorful and specific language.

Product specifications and technical data alone don't move buyers to action, unless it's a firm buyers are already sold on. Persuasive language does. Copy should paint a picture in readers' minds of what the product can do for them. For example:

> Spiral slicing of bone-in hams makes them easier to serve, hot or cold. Great for a buffet supper! Delicious on our home-baked Wheat Grain Bread or in a ham-and-cheese omelette made with our Aged Vermont Cheddar.

> The E-Z dispenser not only lets you carry all your prescription pills with you, but automatically dispenses the right dosage each time you take your medications. It's like having a personal physician and pharmacist right in your pocket!

A Lands' End catalog shows winter gloves made of Polartec, preceded by the headline:

> Nothing as Cozy as Fleecy Polartec!

The description continues:

> Talk about a miracle fabric! Polartec's a superior polyester fleece that's cuddly, soft, lightweight, yet warm as wool, insulates even when wet. Perfect for a person like you who loves frolicking outdoors in the wintertime. (And perfect in someone's Christmas stocking.)

Be specific. Many catalog marketers describe their product as "the fastest," "the lowest cost," "the most efficient," or "the best performer" when they don't really know how their product compares to others on the market. Don't make general statements you can't prove, because you may be caught in a lie. Even if you aren't, buyers distrust general statements. Say, "loads the program in 2.5 seconds" or "price reduced to $495.95" or "detects moisture down to 3 parts per million." Make specific, true claims, and people will believe you.

3. Write powerful headlines and subheads.

Even if space requires your catalog headlines to be short, they can still be powerful sales tools. Write headlines or subheads that go beyond labeling the product, like "A Musical Cuckoo Clock" or "Handblown Glass Tree Ornament."

In its order-by-mail book catalogs, Boardroom Books turns mundane book titles into strong, hard-selling catalog headlines. For a book entitled *The Book of Tax Knowledge*, they write "3,147 Tax-Saving Ideas." For *Successful Tax Planning*, the catalog description reads, "Did your accountant ever tell you all of this?" And a book on how to buy a computer is advertised with the provocative headline, "What the computer salesmen *don't* tell you."

Don't settle for headlines or subheads that are merely labels for the product ("Gear Drive," "Series 2000 Hose Reels," "Spiral Ultrafilter"). Instead, put some persuasion into your headlines. State a benefit. Promise to solve a problem. Mention the industries that can use the product. Tell its applications. Describe the range of sizes, colors, or models available. Give updates about the product. Or stress the ease of product evaluation and selection in your catalog. Examples:

> Widest selection of laboratory stoppers from 1/4" to 1 foot in diameter—in rubber, plastic, glass, and cork.

Color-Coded Floppy Diskettes Save Time and Make Your
Life Easy!

4. Use graphics to draw the reader's attention to appropriate portions of the catalog.

Sensible organization, crisp photography, and powerful copywriting
are the keys to a successful catalog. But experienced catalog marketers
also use graphic devices—boxes, arrows, bursts, underlines, color,
foldouts, varnish on photos, pop-ups—that have little to do with the
basics of salesmanship or good copywriting. Just like a personal letter
from the catalog owner or CEO, these tricks work—and that's reason
enough to use them.

Often used by cereal makers to alert children to the prize inside the
box, the *burst* (a round graphic with a copy line inside) also can draw
a reader to special items within a catalog. Bursts highlight price reduc-
tions, deals, free trials, special features, guarantees, and quantity
discounts.

Use icons to identify items by category or product line. A mail-
order gourmet food catalog, for example, might put little blue circles
next to all items on sale and advertise them as "blue-plate specials."

Use bursts and other special graphic techniques (such as underlining, colored or boldface type, or script) sparingly. Overuse dilutes their
effect.

5. Use photos that demonstrate the product.

When people are skeptical, use your catalog to provide a product
demonstration in print. For example, with cheap brands of computer
paper it's hard to tear off the perforated edges, and sometimes the
printed document rips in the process. Show a photo of how easy your
perforated edges tear away in the user's hand. Or suppose you are selling colored floppy disks on the premise that they are easy to find. Show
a disk holder full of black disks with one bright yellow disk clearly
visible in the middle out of the bunch.

Show the *results* of using the product, not just the product itself. A
recent Day-Timers catalog of appointment books and pocket diaries,
is, as expected, illustrated with photos of products. But instead of
depicting blank books, they show appointment books and diaries filled

with handwritten appointments and entries. This adds realism and believability to the catalog. It shows, for example, how the appointment book could help organize the reader's schedule. If you are selling ab exercisers, don't just picture the machine; show a fit person with rippling abdominal muscles using the device.

6. Make the buyer comfortable with the idea of doing business with your firm.

Business and consumer purchasers want to make the right decision. You can reassure buyers by mentioning firms that have done business with you, testimonials from satisfied customers, and facts that demonstrate the stability of your company (e.g., years in business, annual sales). Many catalogs back up their products with a money-back guarantee, taking the risk out of buying something sight unseen.

Consider listing your business customers. Include a complete or partial list of all the firms that have bought from you, whether you have 30 or 300 names. Seeing such a list in print makes a powerful impression on your customers. They'll think, "How can I go wrong buying from these guys? Everybody in the world does business with them."

7. Show customers how you save them money—or make it.

Saving money provides motivation for a buyer to order your product instead of your competitor's. Your catalog should stress cost savings— on the cover, on the order form, on every page.

In Radio Shack's catalogs, for example, every item is on sale. Each item description lists the price off (in dollars or percentage), the regular price, and the sale price.

A catalog from Boardroom Books shows a markdown on every book in the catalog. The original price is crossed out with an *X,* and the new price is printed next to it in red type.

An office supply catalog from Business Envelope Manufacturers, Inc., announces "Lowest Prices in the Industry" right on the cover.

Let readers know which items are discounted. One way of doing this is to write, "20% Off! Was $9.95—Now $7.95." Another is to cross out the old price and write in the new price: "$9.95. $7.95."

Insert into your catalog a separate sheet featuring any last-minute items and specials—for example, a product that has been reduced in price for inventory clearance. Tell the customer these bargains were included just in time for mailing but too late to print in the catalog. This insert generates additional sales because people like to be "in" on the latest developments.

Catalog copy should show readers how they can make as well as save money by doing business with you. For example, "Telephone Selling Skills That Increase Sales" is a better headline than "Fundamentals of Telephone Sales." The first headline promises wealth; the second is merely descriptive.

8. Include a letter from the president.

Many catalogs include a "personal" letter from the company president, either printed on letterhead and bound into the catalog or printed directly on one of the pages in the front of the catalog. In the letter the president talks about the quality of the products in the catalog, the firm's commitment to serving its customers, and his or her guarantee of customer satisfaction. The letter may also be used as an introduction to the company's product line, as a short history of the company, or to call attention to a particular product or group of products that are especially noteworthy or attractively priced.

Here's a good example of the personal touch from a letter written by the CEO that appeared in an L.L. Bean catalog:

> "L.L." had a simple business philosophy. "Sell good merchandise at a reasonable profit, treat your customers like human beings, and they'll always come back for more." We call this "L.L.'s" golden rule. Today, 72 years later, we still practice it.

You can't help but be won over by the good sense of this honorable business philosophy and the sincerity of its language. Including such a letter in your catalog adds warmth and a human quality to an otherwise impersonal presentation of product facts, specifications, and prices. Nothing builds personality into an ordinary catalog as effectively as a "personal" letter from the company president.

If getting people to warm up to you is your problem—and it might be with new customers or with customers who have been disappointed by your products in the past—you can address the reader directly with a letter on the inside front cover. This letter should be written in a warm, friendly, personal style. And it should be set in typewriter type, not phototype.

9. Add useful information and helpful tips to your catalog.

Adding ancillary information that is useful will encourage buyers to keep the catalog. And the longer they have it, the more often they'll order from it. For instance, a hardware catalog might include an article or table titled, "A Guide to Screw Selection." A filtration catalog could include tips in the section "How to Clean and Care for Filters."

Give the buyer free information that is useful at home or at work. Thomson's 83-page catalog of ball bearings and shafts includes 17 pages on how to select, size, and install the equipment. Engineers will keep the catalog on hand because it contains this helpful information. By adding tips on maintenance, repair, troubleshooting, applications, and operation, you can increase demand for—and readership of—your catalog. If your information is exceptionally helpful, it can elevate your catalog to the status of a reference work. Customers will keep it on their shelves for years.

10. Start selling right on the cover.

Magazine and book publishers put a lot of time and thought into producing attractive, interesting covers for their publications. They know that if a book or magazine has a dull or uninteresting cover, people won't pick it up and buy it. And so it is with your catalog. A bland cover promises a dull recitation of specifications and turns readers off. A cover with an enticing illustration and a strong selling message arouses curiosity and prods a reader to open the catalog.

A catalog is really a "store in a mailbox." The more complete the store, the more likely the customer will return to shop there again and again. A comprehensive product line is a big selling point. Why not stress it on the cover?

Let's say you sell fasteners and have 3,200 product variations. Your competitor's catalog offers only 1,250 models. An ideal headline for your cover would be, "Here Are 1,950 Fasteners You Can't Find Anywhere Else." Underneath would be a photo of some of the fasteners you carry that your competitors don't. Introductory copy on the inside first page would explain the advantages of your broader product line.

Sometimes buyers aren't looking for specific products; they're looking for solutions to problems. You'll win them over if you show how your product solves the problem. For instance, the records administrator at a busy hospital has a problem organizing paper files, finding space to fit the files, and pulling a record quickly when a doctor needs it. This administrator is swamped with paper, but doesn't know what to do. Your microfilm storage system is the ideal solution to this problem, but the records administrator isn't thinking of microfilm. So a cover with the ordinary headline, "A Complete Line of Micrographic Equipment and Accessories" won't sell this reader. A more persuasive headline is "How to Reduce a Mountain of Paper Files to a Neat Stack of Microfiche—and Find Any File in As Little As 15 Seconds." This headline sells a *solution*, not a product.

Product superiority is only one reason why people do business with a company. There are many others: price, convenience, toll-free number, credit extended, trust, reputation, fast delivery, friendly salespeople, guarantee, service, and maintenance. You can generate interest in your catalog by selling both these services and intangibles—on the cover.

When product maintenance is as important as the quality of the product itself, stress your firm's service and support. Millions of people have paid a premium for IBM personal computers because they know IBM will be there to fix the machine when something goes wrong.

Stressing your guarantee is another way of selling service commitment. Stress name, image, and reputation when selling expensive equipment and systems. Buyers want to know that you have the resources to support your systems for years to come, and that you'll be around at least as long as the product lasts. Phrases such as "money-back guarantee!" or "one-year maintenance on all products" concisely convey this message.

One clever approach sometimes used is to start your catalog copy right on the cover instead of using the cover as a mere "introduction." This is an effective way of drawing the reader inside. Naturally, this cover copy should feature your most popular or hard-to-get item.

Consider using a wrapper to make your cover stand out. Wrappers are used to "shout" a sales message. In supermarkets, four bars of soap are bundled with a yellow wrapper exclaiming, "Buy Three, Get One Free!" And this technique is even working its way into bookstores: Stephen Fox's book on the history of advertising *(The Mirror Makers)* was wrapped with a banner singing its praises from David Ogilvy and Rosser Reeves.

The same technique can be applied to catalogs. If you've got a great new product, a discount, or a major improvement in service, delivery, or reliability, announce it with a bright banner wrapped around the cover. Wrappers are also used to announce to buyers that their name will be taken off the mailing list and they will receive no further catalogs unless they place an order. People who enjoy getting your catalog but haven't bought in a while will often place an order just to continue getting the publication.

11. Add value to the product.

Nixdorf Computer's *Solutionware* software catalog offers many of the same programs as other software catalogs. The difference? Nixdorf has created a powerful list of seven "extras" you get when ordering from their catalog. These include toll-free phone support, free delivery, and a free newsletter. This list of goodies appears at the beginning of the book and is repeated on the order form. Readers know they get more for their money when they buy their programs through *Solutionware* instead of another catalog or computer store.

12. Create an inviting order form.

To increase response, make the order form simple and easy to complete, allowing the customer sufficient space to fill in the order. Print step-by-step instructions for ordering right on the form. Print the guarantee in large type and set it off with a border. Provide a business reply envelope in which the customer can enclose a check. Include the names of credit cards accepted, additional charges for shipping or tax, and numbers for ordering by phone or fax.

13. Help the reader shop.

Compatibility is a big problem when selling computer-related equipment and software. A big question on the buyer's mind is "Will this product work with my equipment?" In an otherwise ordinary computer supply catalog, Transnet gives it readers a bonus with a two-page "diskette compatibility chart." The catalog lists the major brands and models of microcomputers alphabetically. Uncertainty and confusion are eliminated. The buyer can place orders with confidence.

Turn your catalog into a "shopping system." A catalog is more than a book of product descriptions; it's a one-stop shopping center for your complete product line. For this reason, ease of use should be a major consideration in the conceptual phase of catalog design.

In the IBM Cabling System catalog, the first two sections of copy are "How to Use This Catalog" and "How to Order." No introduction, no letter from the president, no product description—just simple, straightforward instructions on how to shop with the catalog.

Another helpful touch is to have the price list printed opposite the order form, so the buyer doesn't have to search through the catalog to find prices for the items being ordered.

CHAPTER NINE
Press Releases and Press Kits

P ublicity is news. A press release is picked up by the media because it contains news of interest to a number of readers, viewers, or listeners—not because it is meant to persuade people to buy something. But persuasion is the advertiser's purpose. So in writing a press release the copywriter's goal is to strike a balance between making it persuasive enough to get advertising sales results and giving it enough interesting news content so that a reporter or editor will not reject it as fluff.

Most people don't realize that many news stories appearing in the media have been generated by press releases. Reporters and editors can't possibly cover every story in person. They rely on press releases to generate ideas for articles.

By alerting the media to newsworthy events, products, services, and people, you can prompt a reporter to cover everything from the opening of a new restaurant to the publication of a new catalog, from the techniques of an acupuncturist to the makings of a new trend.

In this chapter you'll learn what a press release is, how to organize and write one, some rules for effective style, and what the format should be. You'll also learn what a press kit is and how to create one, as well as how to write a public service announcement (PSA) and a press "backgrounder."

Press Releases
Rule 1. Use proper press release format.
A press release is a short article distributed to the media in hopes of gaining publicity. Press releases are formatted in a way that makes them

easily identifiable, and are organized in a way that makes them easy for reporters to write from.

Like most news stories, press releases must get to the point quickly, contain news of interest to a large segment of the media's audience, and be attention-catching enough to entice editors to run them.

Generally, press releases follow a standard format. The company name, the contact name, and the contact's phone number are positioned prominently at the top. The words "For immediate release," "Release at your convenience," or "Release date" appear several spaces underneath the company name and several spaces above the headline. If the release is being submitted beyond your locality, include a "dateline" before the first sentence of your release. The dateline consists of the city and state in capitals (e.g., New York, NY).

Your release should be typed double-spaced on one side of white 8 1/2-by-11-inch paper and have wide margins and a headline in caps or boldface. If your copy runs beyond one page, type "MORE" centered at the bottom of each page except the final one.

Starting with page two, number the pages in the upper right-hand corner. At the bottom of the last page of the release, type ### to indicate the end.

Rule 2. Organize news releases in an inverted pyramid.

A press release is usually made up of a headline, a lead, and the body of the story.

Headlines must be concise and present the most significant point in the story in an attention-grabbing style.

The lead should include the *who, what, when, where,* and, often, the *how* and *why* of the story. Journalists traditionally write news stories with the "inverted pyramid" in mind: Their first paragraph summarizes the whole story, and succeeding paragraphs are progressively less vital. When there is not sufficient space for the entire story, the editor cuts from the bottom, knowing that even if only the first paragraph remains intact, the story will be told. Here, for example, is the lead sentence of a lengthy story in the financial section of a newspaper:

> The American Standard Companies said yesterday it had received an unsolicited takeover offer worth 44 billion from

Tyco International Ltd. more than a month ago but that it had rejected the overture and prefers to remain independent.

This sentence encapsulates the key point of the whole article.

Rule 3. Use appropriate style.

The style of a press release depends on the story and the copywriter's unique take on it. For a press release identifying the ten most deadly phrases in business writing, you might use a humorous approach reminiscent of David Letterman's "Top Ten" lists.

NEW SURVEY LISTS TOP TEN PHRASES USED BY BANAL BUSINESS WRITERS

Are your memos and letters crammed with corporate clichés? Here's a list of ten words and phrases to start striking from your next missive:

1. Enclosed please find

2. Under separate cover...

For a press release on an event such as a crafts fair or the giving of an award, use a factual style. The crafts fair release could emphasize the variety of the work displayed and the special nature of each artist's work. The award piece could focus on the biographical details of the recipient and how those details are consistent with the goal of the award.

Rule 4. Find a hook, angle, or theme for your release.

Your release will attract more attention if you have a special hook or angle. The opening of an exhibit that celebrates 90 years of flight would allow the copywriter to exploit the angle of how far flight has come since the days of the Wright brothers. For a release about a noted acupuncturist, one publicist, trying to find a news hook, remembered it had been 25 years since Nixon had renewed relations with China. The press release discussed the acupuncturist within the context of the changes in Chinese-American relations and cultural exchanges.

An *angle* is a special way of viewing a topic. For example, a travel agency trying to promote trips to Paris emphasized a tour of the Paris sewer systems in its release. It worked! A press release discussing a new production of the Arthur Miller play *The Crucible* might well discuss how the play has found a worldwide audience in the 40 years since it was written as a protest against McCarthyism.

Not all the information in a press release has to relate to the angle, however. For example, a release featuring the lighting of a corporate Christmas tree might emphasize the ongoing tradition of the event and may then go on to discuss civic activities engaged in by company personnel during the holidays.

Rule 5. Let the medium dictate the content and tone of your message.

Learn everything you can about the publications you send your releases to. Study current and back copies of magazines and newspapers, see what types of stories are run, and try to figure out where your story could fit. What are the space requirements? Is there a special section appropriate for your release? For example, if you are looking to place news briefs, see if there's a section that runs them. Note the names of the editors of such sections. Be aware of how often newspapers are published (daily, weekly, etc.) and determine how that will influence the chances of their running your story.

For radio and TV, you will send releases to either the news or talk show's managing editor or assignment editor. To gain the attention of a TV producer or editor for your release on an art exhibit, dance recital, or graduation, you may have to include a videotape, photographs, or other evidence that the story is universal, timely, and important.

Rule 6. While playing down any sales aspects, play up the news aspects of your release.

If an editor thinks your release is an attempt to get free advertising, your story will never get printed. Put news in each news release you write. Releases must contain a message of value to the publication's readers.

Compare the two examples below. The first is written with an advertising slant, the second with a news approach.

According to Mr. Smith,
corporate clients recognize
that a helpful voice on the
telephone translates into
happier customers and increased profits.

According to Mr. Smith, his telephone technique
seminars are overbooked because companies
recognize the wisdom in spending training
dollars to have their customer service people
communicate the right corporate image.

The more your copy sounds like news, the better.

Rule 7. Make headlines concise, relevant, and attention-getting.

Headlines are the store-window display of your news release. They summarize what is in the body copy. Also, they should catch the reader's attention. The maximum length of your headline should be two lines.

Here are examples of successful press release headlines:

NEW POSTER COMBATS SEXISM IN THE WORKPLACE

TAPPING THE 'ELF' IN 'SELF' HELPS COMPANIES BUILD TEAM
SPIRIT, MORALE, AND CREATIVITY WHILE REDUCING STRESS

AFTER 50 YEARS, *WONDERFUL LIFE* STILL RINGS TRUE FOR MANY
AMERICANS

NEW PHOTOGRAPHY EXHIBITION EVOKES OLANA, HOME OF
AMERICA'S GREATEST LANDSCAPE ARTIST, FREDERICK CHURCH

Rule 8. Give your story a sense of immediacy.

While trade journals will often publish stories weeks or even months old, the time limitations of TV, radio, and daily newspapers favor events that have an immediacy to viewers and readers.

One way to give releases a sense of immediacy is to tie them in logically with current events. For instance, the publisher of a financial newsletter on platinum tied his promotion to an upcoming election for the presidency of Russia. The theme was that the price of platinum would be affected dramatically by the outcome of the election, because Russia is one of the few major platinum-producing countries in the world.

Rule 9. Use quotations to add color to your release.

Quotations from people involved in the story give your release a liveliness and real-life flavor. In the press release written to promote an acupuncturist's practice ("Ten Years After Normalization of Relations with China, American Acupuncture Comes of Age"), the acupuncturist summarized American attitudes toward acupuncture with a quote that was both colorful and showed contrast, adding to the release's news interest:

> "Ten years ago, when you said 'acupuncture' to an American, he reacted as if you had said 'voodoo.' Today, millions of Americans visit acupuncturists for a variety of ills, and they do so with less fanfare—and a good deal less pain or anxiety—than when they visit their dentist," said Lo Sing, Doctor of Acupuncture.

Quotations not only support the story but, when attributed to real people, entice an editor to run it.

An editor probably would not want to run a press release in which the writer praised the product or service, because this would be editorializing in a news story. But when you include praise for your product or service in an attributed quotation, the editor is more likely to run it. After all, it may be debatable whether the content of the quotation is true, but it is a fact that someone said it. The person you quote could be a representative of your company who praises a newly released product. The following release from Plato Software illustrates this and some other principles of creating effective press releases.

PLATO Software
CONTACT: Richard Rosen, phone 914-246-6648
3158 Rt. 9W
Saugerties, NY 12477

For immediate release

NEW ACCOUNTING SOFTWARE PACKAGE HAS UNIQUE FEATURE: CAN BE MODIFIED BY USERS TO FIT THEIR BUSINESS PROCEDURES AND OPERATIONS

Saugerties, NY—Plato Software has just released the new version of its modifiable business and accounting software package, P&L—Pro Version 2.0.

"What makes P&L-Pro unique is that it's the only affordably priced accounting software that can be modified by the user with no programming required," claims Richard Rosen, president of Plato Software.

"Most low-end, off-the-shelf business software forces you to adjust your business procedures to accommodate the limitations of the program," says Rosen. "As a result, you cannot get the software to do things your way. Some high-end business software packages are designed to be modifiable, but these start at $5,000 to $7,000 and up for a complete system."

P&L-Pro, by comparison, is a complete and affordably priced business and accounting software package that can be modified by users, even non-programmers, to precisely fit their procedures and operations. Cost is approximately $100 per module.

How P&L-Pro Works

Most business software, according to Rosen, is created using complex programming languages, and therefore can only be altered by computer programmers.

P&L-Pro, however, was built using Alpha Four, an easy-to-use database management system. As a result, users can add functions to or modify their copies of P&L-Pro directly, without help from a programmer or software consultant.

The new version, P&L-Pro 2.0, features faster General Ledger posting, simplified setup, better-looking screens, and optimized performance. It also includes two new modules, Payroll and Inventory Control, which—added to the existing modules of General Ledger, Accounts Receivable, and Accounts Payable—make P&L-Pro a complete business and accounting software package that is fully modifiable by the user.

The Payroll module includes all state and federal tax tables and features multiple pay types, unlimited deduction types, and time-card entry. It is completely interfaced with the P&L-Pro General Ledger module. A special feature enables the user to print checks for the new year while printing W-2 forms for the prior year.

The Inventory Control module generates an unlimited number of sales and inventory reports. These reports give the user an up-to-the-minute picture of inventory by product, stock number, location, or any other selected criteria. The module handles purchase-order entry, receiving, sales-order entry, and shipping. And it can be easily customized to fit any method of inventory management and control.

P&L-Pro 2.0 with all five modules sells for $495. A non-modifiable version is available for $249. To order, or for more information, contact: PLATO Software, 3158 Route 9W, Saugerties, NY 12477, phone 800-SWPLATO (800-797-5286), fax 914-246-7597.

###

Press Kits

Press kit is a general term for a press release plus auxiliary materials that accompany and support the release. Press kits are created by companies that wish to establish an ongoing relationship with the media. A press kit may include a fact sheet, biography, a backgrounder, product description, photographs, and a wide assortment of other literature, depending on the purpose and subject matter of the promotion.

Backgrounder. A *backgrounder* fills in the history of a company, highlighting its achievements. It is written to strengthen a firm's reputation and to give the media additional facts about the organization. It can include brief biographies of the founders and company officers, the organization's goals and accomplishments, quotations and even miscellaneous facts that may capture media attention.

Here's a typical page from a backgrounder on a public radio station in New York:

Backgrounder: WABA

WABA—founded in 1945 by John Dundy. During its first 20 years of broadcasting, the station specialized in classical music and public affairs programs. In 1980, it inaugurated a series of Young People's Concerts, under the direction of Milos Karpathian.

- 50,000 watt station

- First classical music radio station in New York City

- 1994—A major archive of recordings was broadcast to a new generation of listeners

- In 1995, Tom Jallow, manager of WABA—AM, FM, and TV— put together a new management team aimed at making WABA one of the top radio and TV outlets in the United States. WABA started raising funds for the upgrading of facilities and equipment, the hiring of first-rate production talent, and the creation of daring and original radio and TV programming.

Through the WABA Foundation, Mr. Jallow and his staff are seeking funds for the expansion of Channel 31's offerings as well as development of WABA's four cable TV stations. Says Jallow, "A new transmitter atop the World Trade Center will soon make our FM and TV signals stronger and clearer. Expansion of our record programs will bring hard-to-find performances and unusual musical pleasures from around the world. A radio facility is in the final design stages. In short, we're becoming the kind of outstanding arts, news, and public service station that all New Yorkers deserve."

Quotes Sheet. Since reporters like to pepper their news stories with lively quotations, companies often provide quotations from executives commenting on the product, service, or event under discussion. While quotations can be incorporated into press releases, a quotation sheet gives reporters greater latitude in choosing quotes to fit the story.

Bios. Biographies of key people associated with your news story are valuable additions to a press kit. Bios should be concise and include information that is pertinent to the topic being publicized.

Brochure. If a release is about a new product, a brochure that explains the product fully will give reporters a better understanding of how the product works and how it can be used. Some brochures may be sales literature that has already been created, but at other times, you may want to boil down certain sales points to fit the style and length of the press kit.

Annual report. Annual reports contain details about how a company operates as well as about a company's performance and are therefore often added to a press kit to round out the other information.

Photos. Photos capture attention, so include product shots and any other photos that will help a reporter illustrate your story.

Public Service Announcements

Public service announcements (PSAs) on radio and television are a common form of publicity. Since they are short, broadcasters run a lot of them, often in 10-, 20-, or 30-second segments. A PSA is an announcement regarded as serving a community interest for which no air-time charge is made. PSAs promote programs, activities, or services of nonprofit organizations and federal, state, and local governments.

On radio, a live spot, which means an announcer reads your copy live on the air, is least expensive. Often, however, PSAs are prerecorded. If you are lucky enough to have a production budget, you can submit your PSAs on tape. Here are a few tips on making your PSAs as effective as possible:

- Use sound effects, music, and dramatic dialogue, not simply a voice. Even if you have not dramatized your spot, consider using two voices. It will sound less monotonous, and your spot will be livelier. The numerous Stiller and Meara radio spots add humor to sales messages and make them more memorable, as do other spots that use sound effects and familiar music to make their messages gain attention and be easily recalled.

A televised PSA on tax amnesty begins with sounds suggesting New Year's Eve—noisemakers, champagne, "Auld Lang Syne"—and makes the point that one of your New Year's resolutions should be to pay back taxes during an amnesty that ends on January 31. The final image is a police blotter, on which are written the words: "Your last chance for a second chance."

- For TV PSAs, use at least one visual for each five to ten seconds in your spot. By using a visual for each five to ten seconds, the station can change images fairly rapidly, and your PSA will have the illusion of motion. This is essential to keeping your audience interested. Both audiotaped and videotaped PSAs should always be accompanied by a script.

- Follow PSA style requirements. Scripts for public service spots should never say "news release" or "for immediate release." If you are sending them in ahead of the time you want them aired, use a heading such as: "Use between April 5 and May 2, 1998."

  Words to be emphasized should be underlined, but don't overdo it. Any difficult name should be followed by its phonetic spelling in parentheses.

- Grab attention. Find a way to make your message fascinating. Think of how your message will benefit your listener. Start with a strong statement of that benefit—a short sentence or two that appeal directly to your listeners' self-interest ("What if tomorrow the hospital in your neighborhood closed down?"). Then follow that with some "who, what, where, when, and how" facts. Conclude by telling the audience what you want them to do: call you, write you, come to an event, send a donation, or just change their thinking on an issue.

  A PSA on drinking and driving concludes with the phrase: "Friends don't let friends drive drunk."

  A PSA on child care concludes: "It's 10 P.M. Do you know where your children are?"

- Don't say too much. Use only one main point in a spot that is 30 seconds or shorter and make sure everything else supports, clarifies, and elaborates on it. In a 60-second PSA, you can sometimes manage to include two points, but they should be related. Every word has to carry meaning.

Read your copy aloud and time it. Try not to say too much; even a professional announcer may have trouble cramming all your copy into the time slot.

End on a forceful note. Keep the closing of the PSA focused and simple. Be single-minded. Be strong. Often, the last line should be a call to action.

Here's the script for a public service announcement produced by the Advertising Council. It appeals to people who are concerned about ecology or interested in the chain of events that cause ecological problems.

A fish died. Because it couldn't breathe. Because its gills got clogged with silt. Because mud ran into the river. Because there was nothing to trap the rain. Because all the trees were gone. Because someone got careless with fire. So please be careful with fire. Because.

A PSA on using seat belts uses no dialogue at all. It shows two eggs, each "seated" in a minicar. One egg is buckled up, the other isn't. When the cars start racing and suddenly stop, the egg that isn't wearing a seat belt is thrown forward and splatters. The last image in a sign saying "Buckle Up."

A PSA for AIDS shows the words "NY Talks AIDS" followed by a teenager talking on screen: "There's someone in your family, your neighborhood, your town who needs help." The last image is the words "Do It!"

CHAPTER TEN

Audiovisual Promotions

The scripting of audiovisual promotions—everything from TV and radio commercials to multimedia presentations —requires that the copywriter's work share the limelight with other elements such as music, film, animation, special lighting effects, computer graphics, or a combination of any of these.

TV Commercials

In his book *How to Produce an Effective Television Commercial*, Hooper White states, "The television commercial...a combination of sight and sound that moves to impart fact or evoke emotion...is one of the most potent selling tools ever forged."

This unique blending in a TV commercial of images and words, camera effects and casting, exposition and dialogue, requires a less sequential and more a visual imagination to achieve its purpose.

Average viewers are bombarded with more than 300,000 commercials a year. To be memorable, a commercial must boil a sales pitch down to one simple, compelling message. The repetition of the message, regardless of the overall effectiveness of the commercial, will usually help produce sales results. No wonder that some successful TV commercials—for everything from car-rental companies to tuna fish—have remained on the air for years.

Although most commercials are forgettable, the few that succeed are noticed and can bring acclaim and fortune to the copywriters who contribute to them. Although the public may not know the name of the person who wrote "We do it all for you," or "Don't leave home without it," or "Just do it," ad agencies and their clients prize writers who can deliver universally memorable copy.

The following are rules for writing copy for TV commercials.

Rule 1. Make a single selling point in a memorable way.

When writing a TV commercial, you are telling a story enhanced by graphics and sound. Where would the copy for the United Airlines commercials ("Come Fly the Friendly Skies") be without the footage of the soaring 767 or the bracing orchestral underscoring of the final bars of Gershwin's *Rhapsody in Blue*? How bland and one-dimensional the slogan for the Beef Council ("Beef—It's what's for dinner") would be without the enticing footage of barbecued steaks and smiling families coupled with the joyous, down-home feeling evoked by the strains of Copeland's *Rodeo*.

Commercials are aimed at a mass audience, and the message must be clear, simple, and direct. If you can make your point using words, images, and sounds that lodge themselves in viewers' minds, you stand a chance of having people remember the brand name of a toothpaste, car, perfume, or computer when the time comes to make a purchasing decision.

Your copy should represent the way you'd like your audience to view your product. Do you want to suggest boldness ("Tap the Rockies: Coors Light"), competence ("We're American Airlines: Doing What We Do Best") or playfulness ("Meow Mix: The Only Cat Food Cats Ask For by Name")? To confront the possible uncertainty of how an audience would respond to a commercial for a Kosher hot dog, Hebrew National met the double challenge by playing to its religious connotation while establishing its value as a food ("We're Hebrew National...and have to answer to a Higher Authority").

Rule 2. Use slogans that bear repeating.

Sometimes you feel like a nut, sometimes you don't.

Chunky: What a chunk of chocolate!

Melts in your mouth, not in your hands.

These slogans have been cleverly wedded to images of their respective chocolate, which are linked with our desire for choice. Think of your product in terms of contrast with the competition and see if you can find the phrase that epitomizes what the product is all about. For Ford Motor Company, the slogan "Quality Is Job One" became an oft-repeated sales message in commercials and print ads. The pun within a slogan like "Milk: It Does A Body Good" makes it the type of slogan that is easy on the ears over a long period of time.

Rule 3. Associate your product with a time of day or week, a specific activity, or a place.

It's Miller time.

Weekends were made for Michelob.

Baseball and Ballantine.

Down in the valley of the Jolly Green Giant.

Marlboro Country.

Rice-a-Roni: The San Francisco treat!

The beer slogans are embellished with video images displaying the camaraderie of blue-collar workers enjoying a well-deserved after-work beer with friends. By associating a particular time of day with your product, you build an emotional association in your reader's mind, an association which may make the product come to mind automatically at the particular time of day.

Rule 4. Use rhyming, especially unusual rhymes, to attract attention.

Take tea and see.

Bounty Towels—the quicker picker-upper!

Aamco—our mission is transmission.

Stop sufferin', take Bufferin.

Winston Tastes Good Like a Cigarette Should.

The fact that the word *like* is grammatically incorrect raised a debate between proper-usage sticklers and advocates of colloquial usage—a debate that just made Winston's commercial even more memorable to those hearing it!

Rule 5. Use puns and double entendres to enhance a routine message.

Calvin Klein: "Nothing comes between me and my Calvins."

American Airlines: Something Special in the Air (Suggests that they are special while flying but simultaneously alludes to the common redolent phrase *something in the air.*)

Burger King: We do it all for you! (States that they do everything and simultaneously suggests that everything is done just for us.)

Virgin Airlines—Take us for all we've got.

Varig Airlines: Brazil on a higher plane.

Advanta Mortgage—We give you the credit you deserve.

By coming up with a phrase that carries two or more messages simultaneously, you tickle the viewer's mind and ear by sending out various connotations, some of which may be an aid in remembering the product's name and may lead to increased sales.

Rule 6. Create an original image in the viewer's mind.

Kentucky Fried Chicken—It's finger-lickin' good!

Listerine kills germs by the millions.

Maxwell House: Good to the very last drop

Many people remember things better if they can visualize an image instead of just words. That's why you need to think in terms of what the product does and create an image that exemplifies the product doing its job. A humorous or even absurd touch can help solidify an image in the mind:

Roach Motel: Roaches check in—but they don't check out.

Rule 7. Separate a product from its competition by creating a lively character or spokesperson for it.

Think of Tony the Tiger, Mr. Clean, the Jolly Green Giant, the Wise Old Owl, Speedy Alka-Seltzer, Charlie Tuna, Joe Isuzu, or corporate executives such as Lee Iacocca, Dave Thomas of Wendy's, or the late Orville Redenbacher, whose personalities shaped their commercials as well as their products.

Is there a person—real or imaginary—that could present your product or service well?

Should the company CEO try to present an image of credibility, as did Lee Iacocca or Frank Perdue? Should the character be animated, like the Wise Old Owl, to associate the product name (Wise) with a quality (wisdom)? You might want to consider a spokesperson whose image somehow reinforces the message you are trying to communicate. Bowery Savings Bank chose Joe DiMaggio as its spokesperson, probably because the Hall of Famer suggested the flavor of New York City as well as the message that, as a longtime retiree, DiMaggio had saved his money wisely.

Rule 8. Show your product as it's being used.

The transformation or before-and-after image—whether it's the cleaning of a greasy pot or the transformation of split ends to silky hair—is a staple of the TV copywriter's craft. The before and after images of shampoo commercials help demonstrate visually that the product does carry out its claims.

Radio Commercials

"Radio reaches more people, more often, than any other medium," says advertising author Grey Smith. No other medium, save theater, can stir the imagination as does radio. No matter what selling approach you use—humor, spokesperson, slice of life, or news—radio still commands one of the most important marketing approaches available to an advertiser, large or small. The intimacy of radio, which reaches millions of drivers, people at work, homemakers, entrepreneurs, and shut-ins, ensures its continuing popularity among advertisers.

Rule 1. Determine what vital information your listener requires and include it.

The most common lengths for radio commercials are 30 and 60 seconds. In those tiny spaces of time, the copy of a radio "spot" should spell out such things as:

- The name of the product and its function

- Features and benefits

- Where or how the product is available

- Position or image the commercial must convey

- Track record of successful experience or use

- Tone (e.g., humorous, serious)

Rule 2. Type your copy in proper radio copy format.

Radio copy is written in ALL CAPITAL LETTERS. Numbers, like 555-1212, are always spelled out: FIVE-FIVE-FIVE, ONE-TWO-ONE-TWO. If a word or phrase is hard to pronounce, it is written out phonetically. Radio copy is always double-spaced. There are 20 lines of copy to the commercial minute, 10 lines of copy in a 30-second commercial, 5 lines of copy in a 15-second commercial, and 3 lines of copy in a 10-second spot.

Radio copy is typed with a wide margin on the left. There is usually a line that goes down the page, with small numbers from 1 to 20 double-spaced, next to the line. There is usually an inch of space to the left of the numbers. This area is used for sound effects (SFX) directions and announcer (ANN) cues. ANN cues are used when there is more than one person performing in the commercial.

Rule 3. Repeat vital information.

A wise radio station sales manager was once asked what makes for a successful radio commercial. He replied, "Name, name, name, name, name, name." In a 60-second spot you should mention the name of the product at least six times. This may appear redundant, but it's not. "One of the best name-recognition radio spots I've ever written mentioned the name 26 times in 60 seconds," says Grey Smith.

This is good advice because many people listen to the radio while driving and, therefore, can't write things down. So repetition to get the name in their minds is essential. Also, many who listen at home do so while occupied by other things and do not have pencil and paper handy. If you do want them to write something down, tell them to "have pencil and paper handy" early in the commercial, before giving the vital details, such as an address or a toll-free phone number.

Rule 4. Catch your listener's attention quickly.

There are as many ways to begin a commercial as there are products and services to sell, but a commercial must have a hook if it is to work. And the hook must catch the listener in the first 10 seconds, otherwise he won't be caught in the remaining seconds. In a radio commercial for Buckley's Mixture, your attention is gained by the fact that the advertiser admits their cough syrup tastes terrible! They promote its effectiveness by making the logical connection in the listener's mind that if medicine tastes bad, it must be strong—and it must work. They back this up with the fact that Canadians, who live in colder climates than Americans, are experts in handling coughs, and Buckley's is the best-selling cough syrup in Canada. They end the spot with the slogan "Buckley's Mixture—it tastes terrible, and it works."

Consider also the emotional mood or approach that you intend to use to grab and keep the listener's attention. You can be friendly, satiric, clever, dignified, silly, or sentimental.

When you finish writing your copy, read it aloud. Copy that looks structurally good on paper may not sound natural when spoken. It may sound awkward or stuffy. Spoken language isn't always delivered in perfect, complete sentences. It uses sentence fragments and exclamations. Write your copy the way you talk

Rule 5. Stretch the listener's imagination.

Voices and sounds can evoke pictures in the mind. Take your listeners somewhere they've never been before or somewhere they'd like to go. Jungle sound effects, for example, quickly underscore the exotic nature of travel through the jungles of Africa or South America.

Rule 6. Select your customers quickly.

Get the attention of the particular customers you want to reach—and flag them down quickly before they have a chance to change stations. Beginning a commercial with the question "Bothered by an itchy scalp?" can immediately catch the attention of those listeners who suffer from this ailment.

Rule 7. Capitalize on local events.

Tie in with fads, fashion, news events, weather, or holidays. Obviously, chocolate retailers tie in their product with Valentine's Day and common cold and flu remedies often are advertised to tie in with the first blast of winter weather.

Rule 8. Ask listeners for action.

You can't make a sale unless you ask for the order. Don't be afraid to ask the customer to try your product or service today. Law firms specializing in accident cases often end with the phrase: "Keep our number handy." *Sports Illustrated* magazine ends their commercials with the ever-popular "Operators are standing by."

Rule 9. Use the strength of radio personalities.

Radio personalities have steady listeners. Have them deliver the radio spot live. Many disc jockeys and show hosts have a strong hold on their audiences. Many personalities, at one time or other, have lent their names to products or read on-air spots, including Bob Hope, Bing Crosby, Imus, Larry King, Jack Benny, Howard Stern, and Sally Jessy Raphael.

Audiovisual Presentations

Just as diverse ingredients blend to form a single, exciting entree, so various media (film, overhead transparencies, flip charts, videos, handout materials) can unite to form an impression that is more potent than any single contributor. Multimedia presentations are a staple of business conferences, proposals, seminars, and sales presentations.

When writing audiovisual presentations, be aware of the relationship between the graphic elements and your copy (e.g., How much copy should accompany each graphic image? How does the boldness of the image affect the way in which the copy should be written?). Also, by being aware of the time, logistical, and budgetary restraints on the copy, a copywriter can include effects that do not require great expenditures of time or money.

A multimedia presentation can be used to instruct or to sell or to convey a mood or tone about a person, place, product, service, or idea.

Rule 1. Write copy for use with media that is appropriate to the purpose, budget, and time limitations of the presentation.

Your copy may be written for the owner of a car dealership or satisfied customers of a clinic, pet store, furniture outlet, or mortgage company. Or perhaps your words will be embellished only by other words flashed on the TV screen—800 numbers, "Call Now!" or "Sale Ends Tuesday!" In any case, you should match the words to the overall image of the advertiser, which may be homey, small townish, flashy, or subdued. The purpose may be to get people into a store or dealership immediately. Therefore, the words must leave no doubt as to the benefits and limited time of a sale or other offering.

Audiovisual multimedia is often expensive, although it need not be. Prices vary widely. Get competitive quotes.

Major advertisers will spend $100,000 or more to produce one 30-second commercial for the Superbowl. On the other hand, the Hair Club for men, a successful national television advertiser, routinely spends less than $10,000 a spot to make its commercials. Not all of us, however, are called upon to create copy for national TV campaigns; more often, local businesspeople need copy for hometown TV commercials with a tight budget and a limited choice of music, graphics, or other embellishments.

Watch audiovisual presentations with an eye toward how much can be suggested by relatively small resources. While it might be nice to have the services of a Mary Lou Retton or Kathie Lee Gifford to tout the wonders of a new food or fitness product or a cruise line, you might not have the luxury of a star with built-in appeal or credibility. While you may not be able to get Cal Ripkin to sell the trustworthiness of a bank or mortgage company, you can use clever copy and images to achieve potent effects. When trying to adhere to a budget, think in terms of using inexpensive talent, everyday people, and modest props and sets to dramatize your copy.

Rule 2. Take full advantage of the interactivity of on-line formats.

An on-line platform, which includes CD-ROM, software, and Web pages, offers users interactivity—the ability to respond to the material they are viewing through hypertext links and branching. When you're writing for on-line material, take full advantage of its interactive capability.

There are many similarities between copy written for the printed page (e.g., a brochure) and copy for the computer. The difference is primarily in the structure of the presentation. In a brochure you are limited to the linear structure of print, where page three invariably follows page two. But in a CD-ROM presentation, page three doesn't have to follow page two. By clicking on a hypertext link, icon, button, or menu item, the reader can jump from one part of the presentation to another in the manner he or she prefers.

Interactivity can provide fun and stimulating reading. It gets the prospect actively involved with the presentation and the product or service you are selling. For instance, if you are writing a CD-ROM on a new car, let the prospect design his or her dream car by clicking on model options, color, and so on.

Keep it simple. Do not overuse interactivity simply because it's there. Too many choices will make the presentation difficult to use and may confuse the user rather than help. Offer interactive choices where they make sense in the presentation, not at every available juncture.

CHAPTER ELEVEN
The World Wide Web

The growth of the Internet has created a new medium for advertisers and their copywriters: Web pages. As this book goes to press, more than 60 million people worldwide use the Internet, and more than 17 million Americans browse the World Wide Web at least once a week. There are more than 7 million home pages on the World Wide Web. This number is expected to increase to an incredible 1 billion home pages within the next few years.

Let's start with some basics: The *Internet* is a massive network through which computers throughout the world potentially can be connected to every other computer in the world.

The *World Wide Web* is a segment of the Internet. The Web consists of about a million computers, known as *servers*, that store information designed to be accessible to people who *surf* the Web. To *surf*—or navigate or browse—is to look through the files on these computers and find data of particular interest.

The content of the World Wide Web is divided into segments called *Web sites*. Each Web site is accessible using a different code, known as the URL (Uniform Resource Locator). An example of a URL is http://www.bly.com/. This is often called the Web site address. A server containing the text and graphics of one or more Web sites is said to be *hosting* those sites.

The two main elements of any Web site are the *home page* and *Web pages*. The first thing a Web surfer sees when accessing any given Web site is the home page, which functions as a combined table of contents and introduction. Just as the table of contents in a book tells you what you will find on subsequent pages, the home page leads the Web browser to other pages, known as Web pages.

A third element is *hypertext,* which consists of electronic links that help browsers immediately find information of interest to them within or between Web sites. Key words, phrases, concepts, or topics that visitors to the Web site might want more information on are highlighted. Clicking on the word or group of words calls up a Web page that gives more detailed information on that particular subject.

When creating Web pages, keep these demographics about Web users in mind:

- 75 percent are between the ages of 16 and 44.

- 55 percent have incomes over $55,000 a year.

- 54 percent have college degrees, and 26 percent have graduate degrees.

- 7 out of 10 business users browse the Web for production information and evaluation.

- Web surfing by business prospects is projected to double over the next 18 months.

Here are some tips for writing effective copy for this new electronic medium.

1. Determine your objective before you begin to write.

Marlene Brown, an authority on Internet marketing and author of the book *Techno Trends,* offers the following advice as the first step in creating a Web site:

Before you set up shop on the Internet, determine what your objectives are. Do you want to sell your present products? Launch a new one? Market your programs and services? Build traffic on your home page? Clearly determine your objectives, then establish measurable goals as to what will constitute success.

Define your target audience. Where and who are your best prospects? Do you want to advertise your products generically, or target them? Browse through present bulletin boards, join discussion groups, share ideas on mail lists to enable you to see what is in demand, and who wants to buy it.

Surveys are a great way to get information about what Internet people think of your products, especially new ones you may launch, or a series of related products you plan to bundle. Surveys give us ideas on needs and prevent us from wasting time on products for which there are no big markets.

The Web is, in a sense, a low-cost, electronic version of traditional direct marketing. Like traditional direct marketing, Internet marketing can generate a measurable response, and it has the advantages of always being immediate and not requiring any physical materials (e.g., business reply card or order form). But you can't know whether you are getting a good or bad result unless you establish objectives and then measure your results against these objectives.

After your Web site is operational for a few months, you'll have a better idea of what you can realistically expect to achieve, and then you'll be able to adjust your objectives accordingly. At the same time, read articles in the business press to find out the results others are getting with their Web sites. This will help you set a goal to shoot for.

2. Register a domain name people will look for.

The domain name is the key part of the code the Web surfer types to reach your Web site. To reach the Web site of Bob Bly, a coauthor of this book, for example, type http://www.bly.com. The domain name is bly.com.

Your Internet Service Provider (ISP), or whatever firm you select to host your Web site, can register a domain name for you. Choose a domain name that people will be likely to remember. Although there are many easy-to-use *search engines* for finding Web sites by subject matter or source, many Web browsers don't bother to use them, and having to use a search engine to find a particular site because you can't remember the address can be inconvenient.

Users already familiar with your site but who can't remember the address are more likely to type in a few guesses until they hit upon your actual domain name and can access your Web site. For instance, the domain name for the BOC Group, a large industrial manufacturer, is, logically, boc.com. They could have also chosen bocgroup.com. You should choose a domain name that is either identical or close to your company name, or one that relates to the category of product or service you provide. For instance, if you are a large freight forwarder, you might select freight.com or ship.com. If your company name is Global Transportation, you might choose global.com or globtrans.com.

Domain names are unique: If your competitor registers a domain name, no one else can use it. However, you can always register a variation of the name, if that domain name is still available. For example, if barbecue.com is taken, perhaps you will want to register BBQ.com or maybe grill.com—both good choices for a manufacturer of barbecue grills.

3. Use a "Web site under construction" sign.

Since the complete development of the content of your Web site may lag behind the site becoming operational by several weeks or months, you don't want browsers to find it empty. Here's what to do:

Set up on the home page some boilerplate copy about your company and its products and services. Include contact information—phone number, fax number, e-mail address—so people interested in learning more can contact you directly, even though your Web site does not yet have a mechanism for direct response through the Web other than e-mail (it will; see tip 8 in this chapter). You can write custom copy for the site or simply scan, edit, and put on the site existing boilerplate copy from a corporate capabilities brochure, a backgrounder press release, or other existing marketing document.

This noninteractive message puts your message on the World Wide Web until your full Web site is ready, so visits to your site are not wasted. Above this descriptive copy put a box with text in large bold letters that says, "WEB SITE UNDER CONSTRUCTION." This tells visitors to your site that the current state is temporary, so they shouldn't be put off by the lack of functionality, design, and detailed content... all of which are to come.

Interestingly, many ISPs automatically provide 8 Megabytes (MB) of server space for you to have a Web site at no extra charge when you use them to provide your Internet access. Our guess is that there are thousands of ISP customers who have, in effect, paid for server space on which they could put a Web site and don't even know it. As of this writing, even CompuServe customers automatically get 1 MB of server space at no charge.

4. Make your copy modular.

The Web is a truly modular medium in that the information you put up on your Web site must be divided into separate pages or sections.

These pages are electronically connected, but Web browsers need not go through them sequentially. Users can skip from page to page, looking for information of interest.

Write and design your Web site with this in mind. Break the subject of the Web site up into modules, the way you would break a training course into segments or a manual into chapters.

Make the text within each Web page modular as well. Don't design a page with a solid block of text, as in a book. Break it up into four or five sections, each with its own subhead. This is the way Web browsers prefer to digest information—in short, bite-size chunks.

5. Keep it short and simple.

Web pages should be written in plain English; no special language, computer codes, diagrams, or flowcharts should be used in place of conventional sentences and paragraphs.

The beauty of the World Wide Web is that information can be presented and accessed in layers. This is what enables you to keep your Web pages brief while still offering more detailed information to those who are interested.

If there is a difference, aside from hypertext links, between the printed page and on-line writing, it's that Web page copy must be brief. There is no need to make Web pages longer than a page or two, because if there is more detailed information, the Web surfer can be directed, via a hypertext link, to a different page or another site on that topic. Most of your Web pages should be one to one and a half pages long. If the page looks as if it will exceed two pages, break it up into two separate subject pages, and connect them via a hypertext link.

Keep paragraphs in Web pages short. Most paragraphs should be no longer than three to four lines. An occasional longer paragraph is okay, but when in doubt, break long paragraphs into two or more shorter paragraphs.

6. Use internal hypertext links as an on-line index.

In a printed book you turn to the index, look up the subject by name, then turn to the pages where this information is located. With on-line writing, the document itself is its own index. Key words are highlighted and linked via hypertext to other sections of the document.

Do not overdo the links. If every other word is underlined, high-lighted, and hyperlinked, it will confuse or overwhelm Web browsers and they won't click on anything. Highlight only those key topics that you want the prospect to explore further. As a rule of thumb, if you break up a Web page into sections with subtopics separated by sub-headings, you shouldn't have more than one hyperlink per section, or more than four or five per Web page.

7. Use strategic external hyperlinks to increase visits to your Web site.

One type of hyperlink is to connect Web pages within a Web site. But you can also put in hyperlinks that instantly transport your prospect to the home pages of other advertisers or organizations. In return, they hyperlink their sites to your home page.

For example, if you sell pet supplies, it would be natural to link your Web site to the home page of the American Cat Breeders' Association. If you sell desktop publishing software, a link to a Macintosh user's group, such as MacSciTech, makes sense, as would a link to the Apple Computer Web site. You can increase visits to your own site by pointing browsers at these other sites to your own home page.

By arranging these strategic hyperlinks, you improve the use-fulness of your site and others by helping browsers access related information.

8. Give people a reason to complete your enrollment page.

Every business Web site should have an enrollment page. The enroll-ment page is a Web page where visitors to your site can register, giving you key information about themselves, including name, company, title, address, phone, fax, and e-mail.

If you're a Web advertiser, the enrollment page is an extremely valu-able tool. It allows you to more accurately measure Web response, pro-vides a vehicle prospects can use to request additional information, and enables you to build a prospecting database that includes, among other things, prospects' e-mail addresses. Once you have this database, you can target e-mail, fax broadcasts, direct mail, and other repeat promotions at prospects as appropriate.

To get qualified prospects to "register" (fill out) your enrollment page isn't difficult. You simply offer them something of value which they cannot gain access to until they have completely filled out the enrollment page. This can be the ability to:

- Download or request free literature

- Use an on-line calculator or other Web site utility

- Subscribe to an e-mail newsletter or other on-line or printed publication

- Request a price quotation or get some preliminary recommendations

The principle is similar to that used in printed direct mail which includes a reply card the advertiser wants the reader to fill out and mail back. Direct-mail reply cards are filled out and returned only when the prospects are given an incentive to do so, such as a gift, free catalog, free estimate, and so on. Enrollment pages work exactly the same way: Give your site visitors a compelling reason to fill it out, and they will.

9. Add functionality, not just information.

Because Web pages are computer files run on computer systems, they can go beyond the printed page to offer degrees of functionality conventional sales literature cannot match.

For instance, on the home page for Studebaker-Worthington, a nationwide computer leasing company, there is a handy "Quick Quote" calculator you can access. Simply enter the purchase price of the computer system, and the calculator instantly shows you the monthly lease payments.

On the home page for Edith Roman Associates, a large mailing list broker, there is a "Quick Count" calculator you can use to get instant list counts. You enter the type of market you want to reach and the program instantly displays the names of the available mailing lists, the number of names on each list, and the list rental cost. This is a convenient feature for marketing managers who are planning campaigns and need to get a quick idea of the size of potential markets.

If your product or service lends itself to this type of utility, add it to your Web site and make it accessible from your home page. You don't need to make it elaborate or have many of them, but adding a utility makes your Web site more interesting and useful, so that more of your prospects will visit it more often.

10. Change the content periodically and make it clear that you do so.

Another big difference between printed brochures and on-line marketing documents is that the latter can be easily updated at any time with virtually no cost. Printed brochures cannot. With a printed brochure, if you have new information, you either have to reprint the brochure and throw out the old copies, or add an insert sheet or other supplement highlighting the new information (which doesn't delete any dated or wrong information in the old brochure). In either case, it takes time and money.

Advertisers with Web sites find electronic updating to be both a blessing and a burden. The blessing is that on-line marketing documents can always be up-to-date and don't cost anything to revise. The burden is that you're always having to go back into your Web site and to make revisions and corrections as new information becomes available.

Since the content of your Web site is being continually changed and updated, this gives prospects a reason to periodically revisit the Web site to obtain the latest, most accurate information. Let them know this. You can put a message on your home page that says, "Information changes rapidly and the XYZ Company Web site is continually updated. Visit us often to get the most current data."

Another technique is to have a separate section (Web page) dedicated specifically to news and announcements. This bulletin can change monthly, weekly, or even daily. The more often it changes, and the more important the information, the more frequently prospects will visit your site. If you have such an announcements page, feature a link to it on your home page, and include a comment that encourages browsers to visit it on every trip to your site.

11. Use an FAQ.

An FAQ is a unique type of Web page. These pages containing frequently asked questions are extremely important, very popular, and nearly always read. Since the FAQ is a separate Web page, Web surfers can easily download it and even print it for permanent reference. A FAQ page is a way to convey information simply, easily, and quickly. If it weren't for a FAQ, your e-mail would be jammed with people asking the same questions over and over again. In his book *Cyberwriting,* copywriter Joe Vitale offers these suggestions for writing effective FAQs:

- **Be brief.** By now you know that everything you write on-line should be as brief and to the point as possible. There's simply too much happening on-line and too many other posts to read for anyone to spend a great deal of time on your material. Write a clear question and give a direct answer and move on to the next question. Ten lines of text is a reasonable limit for each of your answers.

- **Be lively.** FAQs that simply give "information" can be boring. Spice up your writing. Add eye-opening statistics, engaging stories, stimulating quotes. Make reading your FAQ a delight. Say something that surprises your readers. Add a fact that makes them sit up and say, "I didn't know that!"

- **Provide resources.** Although you aren't writing a term paper or dissertation, your FAQ is a resource for people. Make it a complete one by including details on how to get more information. If you have a list of books, articles, or tapes, include them. If you have a directory of people or places for people to contact for more information, include it. And remember to add your own name, address, phone and fax numbers, and, of course, e-mail address.

- **List questions up front.** It's common practice to list all the questions being answered in your FAQ at the beginning of the FAQ. This way, anyone wanting to know the answer to a particular question can tell at a glance whether you cover it or not.

12. Cross-promote.

Once you have a Web site, promote it heavily. In your ads, mailings, and company newsletter, encourage prospects and customers to visit your Web site. Put your Web site address on every marketing and business document you produce, including letterhead and business cards.

In marketing communications, mention a benefit the prospect will get as an incentive to go to your Web site. For instance, you may have special information that is available only on the Web site and not in other media. Or you may post special sales and discounts on the Web site that are only available at the site. Studebaker-Worthington Leasing Corporation offers cash incentives and merchandise gifts to computer resellers who use their leasing services. They now offer special gifts only available on the Web site, which increases traffic.

Important marketing documents should be published on the Web site, along with other relevant documents offered on the site through the enrollment page, e-mail, or other means.

13. Keep graphics to a minimum.

Graphics add interest, but words communicate the bulk of the information on the Internet. So keep your Web site simple. "Ease of communication and clarity of use should be your targets," says Joe Vitale. "Always aim for simplicity. If your copywriting isn't compelling, few will buy. True, on-line browsers certainly want information, but don't feed it to them in dry chunks. The more you can add emotional excitement to your words, the better your chances of being read, being remembered, and having your services bought."

Vary what you write. Some people create their own paperless documents, such as e-zines, or electronic magazines, and design them for home page use. There are far too many diversions for readers in cyberspace, so don't be boring. With one click they can leave your site and never return.

Keep what you say interesting. Always think of your readers and give them what they want, not what you want. A good rule of thumb in writing any marketing piece is, "Get out of your ego and into the reader's ego." Write what would keep them interested. As advertising executive Howard Gossage once said, "People read whatever interests them, and sometimes it's an ad." Make your on-line text interesting and they just might read what you write.

Be sure to include your name, address, phone and fax numbers, and e-mail address on every page of your Web site documents. You never know when a reader will suddenly want to contact you. Don't make that person backtrack through several layers of hyperlinks just to find out your phone number. Put your contact information at the top (or bottom) of every page.

CHAPTER TWELVE

Other Formats

This chapter will focus on the copywriting of newsletters, invoice stuffers, manuals and instructions, and signs and billboards.

Newsletters

With more than 25,000 promotional and subscription newsletters in the United States, this popular publishing vehicle represents one of the fastest-growing industries of the decade. Newsletters are tied to the information explosion. Readers want specific information. Copywriters need to serve up the information in a crisp, entertaining manner.

There are two basic types of newsletters: subscription and promotional. Subscription newsletters are sold for profit by entrepreneurs for whom the newsletter is their primary source of income. *The Pryor Report*, for example, is a subscription newsletter subscribed to by more than 20,000 busy executives. *Business & Acquisition Newsletter* is a subscription newsletter that advises readers of companies, product lines, and patents available for sale.

Many companies use promotional newsletters that are free or low cost and are distributed to customers, clients, prospects, employees, journal editors, and decision makers in their industries. American Express, for example, includes a small newsletter when mailing cardholders their monthly bills. Fidelity Magellan, a large mutual fund, sends people who have invested in one or more of their funds a free investment magazine. The main purpose of these publications is to establish their company's credibility with a select audience: the people who do business with the company over an extended period of time.

Here are a few rules to guide you in creating effective promotional newsletter copy.

Rule 1. Keep the newsletter—and the stories in it—brief.

Stories in a newsletter can range from a single paragraph to several pages, but most are shorter rather than longer. Unlike a brochure in which each section builds on the previous section, each article in a newsletter is self-contained. Keep your newsletter to eight pages and keep most articles well under 750 words.

Although the order of articles is not critically important, common sense dictates that you put the most important and interesting stories on page one and the others on the inside pages.

Rule 2. Keep articles focused on the readers' interests and information that is useful to them.

Don't try to be everything to everybody. People are interested in self-help and in discovering information that will be useful, profitable, or interesting. Newsletters shouldn't wander too far from providing this type of help. For example, an entire issue of *PR Ink,* a newsletter for PR professionals, was devoted to "How To Pick Press Kit Photos Editors Will Want to Use." This topic is of interest to its readers—PR people at small firms who send press releases to the media—and the article offered helpful information.

The New York metro division of the American Society of Training and Development publishes a newsletter, *Lamplighter,* with articles of interest to human resources managers and training managers. No wonder, then, that an article such as "Conflict Can Be Positive" was featured in it, since this could be of interest to almost every training professional who frequently faces classroom conflict and offered useful information.

Company newsletters should offer articles about products and services of interest to customers and potential customers, as well as ideas and methods for solving the problems that customers have. They should also address news, technology, and other timely information of interest to that audience. The brief newsletters that often accompany airline frequent flyer reports contain articles about ways of earning more mileage or suggestions for using accumulated mileage for low-cost vacations.

Rule 3. Be informal and relaxed.

Although newsletters tend to reflect the tone of their area of interest, we believe your newsletter's articles should have the warmth and tone of the human voice. Write to express, not to impress. Use words that communicate your message clearly and concretely. Don't use any of the lawyerlike language often found in business communication (e.g., *herein, wherein, heretofore, deem it necessary*). Try to avoid the passive voice (e.g., *It is recommended, It is believed*). Feel free to use contractions to warm up your prose. Recognize that some sentences will sound better when they end with a preposition. Use short sentences and short paragraphs. Avoid slang, but use an occasional colloquialism. Some sentences can begin with conjunctions. Except in formal corporate newsletters, you can use *I* or *we*, and even get away with the occasional exclamation point. You can use dashes liberally, italicize text, and even use the occasional parenthetical remark.

A newsletter to Barnes and Noble customers starts a story on children's books: "Calling all toddlers!" A newsletter sent to Fidelity Investments customers achieves a conversational tone by using contractions, starting sentences with conjunctions, and keeping sentences short: "With just one toll-free call on your touch-tone phone, you can buy, sell, or exchange shares of any of these funds without transaction fees. It's quick, convenient, and automatic. And you can call any time it fits into your schedule—day or night...."

Rule 4. Vary the contents.

Too many newsletters make the mistake of providing only one type of article or feature. You need to explore many ways of presenting information to keep hooking your reader. If you use a lot of service pieces—how-to articles on relevant subjects—you might also want to include a letters column that invites comments and ideas from readers.

Other possibilities include a Q&A column, which provides answers to readers' questions; guest articles by qualified specialists; and checklists of do's and don'ts to dramatize the contents of a service piece. In general, 80 percent of your newsletter should be informational; only about 20 percent should be blatantly promotional.

There's no end to topics you can cover in your newsletter. They can include:

- Company news
- Industry news
- New products
- Product improvements
- New models
- New accessories
- New applications
- Troubleshooting guides
- Trends
- Customer profiles
- Quizzes
- Contests
- Announcements and write-ups of conferences, seminars, meetings, and trade shows
- Community relations activities
- Manufacturing success stories
- Recent innovations in research and development
- Case histories

While you may be tempted to write a newsletter the size of an annual report and put it out weekly, resist doing so. We suggest publishing your four- to eight-page newsletter at least three times a year and no more than six times a year. Quarterly is ideal.

Rule 5. Use article titles that promise your reader a benefit or useful information.

In a newsletter, news comes first. Newsletters are read because they deliver news that keeps readers well informed and a step ahead of the competition.

The how-to article is a staple of many newsletters. People want to learn how they can master their environment, and newsletters can fill them in. How-to articles stress not only how to do something but the benefits to be derived.

In a brief article entitled, "'Tis the Season," *The Old Original Bookbinder's Review* (the newsletter of one of Philadelphia's oldest restaurants) mentions that "the holidays are rapidly approaching" and continues with "Need a quick gift idea? Give that someone special a taste of Philadelphia…Old Original Bookbinder's Soup and Condiment Gift Packs!" Though obviously promotional, this article does catch the reader's attention with the promise of information about last-minute gift ideas. Other examples of how-to articles include "Ten Ways to Improve Your Correspondence," "Lower Your Stress Through Exercise," "How To Rent an Apartment" and "Creating a Web Home Page."

Rule 6. Use drawings, photos, bullets, boxes, checklists, and other ways of calling out information.

To keep the reader visually stimulated, break away from prose occasionally. You can use line drawings to illustrate ideas. Photos are appropriate when a picture will capture an image (e.g., what a tattoo looks like) better than words could possibly suggest. You can break up a long block of text with a feature quote—text excerpted from the article which is displayed in a box or between ruled lines. The called-out text draws attention to your article and acts as a type of overall caption for it. Pick up a copy of a favorite magazine and you'll see examples of how designers use feature quotes to add flair to an article's layout.

All photos and drawings should get captions because they get high readership. Use captions to communicate details or to explain ideas, not just as labels (e.g., instead of "TPS-43 radar" write "New parabolic antenna for TPS radar increases detection range by 25%").

Bullets or other dingbats (boxes, stars, triangles) are appropriate when you wish to communicate a list of items, rules, ideas, or directions. Checklists can rivet attention on major ideas contained in an article.

Invoice Stuffers

Invoice stuffers are small pieces of promotional literature designed to fit into regular business envelopes (#10). They are mailed to customers along with the monthly bill or statement and are used to announce a sale or solicit mail orders for a special item. The advantage of using invoice stuffers is that they get a "free ride" in the mail because they're sent with routine correspondence rather than in special mailings.

The invoice stuffer may also be used to notify customers of a new policy; announce a rate increase; remind customers of maintenance or repair procedures they should be doing; sell accessories, additional services, or merchandise; encourage customers to increase usage or spending; or offer an upgrade of an existing product or service.

Rule 1. Design your invoice stuffer to look different from the correspondence it's being mailed with.

If, for example, your invoices are on cream-white paper, print the invoice stuffer on bright yellow stock. If your invoices are 8 1/2-by-11-inch sheets printed on your letterhead, make your stuffer a colorful 4-by-9-inch piece on glossy stock.

Rule 2. Use a direct headline.

Because of space limitations and the fact that the reader is looking at other material in the envelope (and may be quickly scanning through and throwing away a stack of material in other envelopes, including inserts), make your headline direct (see chapter 2). For example: "Charming Miniature Grandfather's Clock…Keeps Accurate Time and Chimes on the Hour…Only Four Easy Payments of $29.95."

Rule 3. Advertise one item per insert.

Inserts work best selling one item at a time. If you have three different specials you want to promote, put three inserts, one for each product, into the statement or invoice envelope for that month.

Manuals and Instructions

Manuals and instructions are made to be used and followed—not ignored because they are cumbersome, poorly written, or obscure.

A clear, easy-to-follow manual can increase productivity, save money, speed acceptance of new procedures, and increase use of a new system. Here are some guidelines for manual writers.

Rule 1. Organize logically.

The best way to organize a manual or instruction sheet is to make an outline. The items in your list will help you stay on course as you explain what readers should do. Use the items in your outline as headings and subheadings. This procedure will help you prepare material that reflects your product's "learning curve" and will break the text into short, easy-to-read sections.

Rule 2. Use numbered, step-by-step instructions.

Clear instructions, given in sequence in a numbered list format, leave no room for doubt. Use the active narrative voice. Start sentences with imperatives, and use direct statements. For example, the manual accompanying a database package guides the reader with these instructions:

Step 1. Type "UNISTOX."

Step 2. Locate the report numbers in Source Digest or Data Reports.

Rule 3. Minimize cross-references.

The overuse of cross-references makes manuals hard to follow. Here's a real-life example:

In order for the FOCUS REPORT Writer (see Section 2.3.1) to read a Total Database (see Database manual), the user or project designer must prepare a FOCUS Data Description (see Section 3.4.1) that is equivalent to the TOTAL database structure (see Appendix C).

Instead of learning the system, users will spend time frantically turning pages, switching from section to section for instructions or descriptions vital to understanding what they're reading.

Too many cross-references can be frustrating and confusing. Use only those cross-references that are absolutely necessary for the reader to understand the material.

Rule 4. Show—don't tell—and use lots of illustrations.

Manual users would rather do than read. The text should be concise and should simply show what to do, rather than give an explanation about a procedure.

When words cannot adequately describe a task, use illustrations to complement the text. For example, in addition to writing "Insert plug A into wall socket B," show a picture of a labeled plug being inserted into a clearly labeled wall socket.

In an instruction sheet entitled "Important Protection Information," National Car Rental Company illustrates key topics with illustrations. For example, information about personal accident insurance is illustrated by a figure in a cast and on crutches. Information about personal-effects coverage is illustrated by a picture of a valise, ski poles, skis, and a radio. "Fuel Purchase Option" is illustrated with the nozzle of a gas pump.

Airline safety instructions are also richly illustrated models of clarity. The safety card used aboard American Airlines flights is a laminated, two-sided, 8 1/2-inch-by-11-inch sheet that is 75 percent illustration and only 25 percent text. The illustrations show, with few accompanying captions, how to buckle a seat belt, put on an oxygen mask, open an exit door, and get into a crouching position for an emergency landing.

To achieve the clear, uncluttered look, manuals should use wide margins and lots of blank or "white" space.

Rule 5. Add guideposts to aid readability.

Another way of keeping the reader on track is adding guideposts—a table of contents, introduction, index, and tabs. The table of contents outlines all the sections and subsections of the manual. The index should cover key terms and concepts but not every word in the manual. If readers want to look up how to copy a computer disk, they should be able to find the entry "Copying disks" in the index.

Rule 6. Test-drive your manual.

The true test of a manual writer's work is whether the directions given can be understood by their intended audience. So give drafts of manuals to people who will routinely use them as a way of determining their effectiveness.

For instance, if a manual helps checking account holders use an automated teller machine, give a draft of the manual to typical checking account customers. If they have trouble following the manual, try to discover what is unclear. If the manual is clear to typical account holders, then the instructions will probably be understood when given to a wide number of these people.

Signs and Billboards

Although the copywriter who writes signs and billboards may be the same person who creates copy for magazine and newspaper advertisements, there are special techniques that have proven to work well for these very noticeable promotions.

Rule 1. Keep It simple.

First, focus on key words. Choose only a few words that describe your business. Clever or strange names may confuse people. Likewise, unclear symbols confuse rather than communicate. The cleaner and clearer the message, the more impact it has.

Second, be brief. Most people will not take the time to read a sign with lengthy copy, so your message can't be long. Billboard readers are usually in a car going 40 or 50 miles per hour and will only glance at your message for a few seconds.

Here are some examples:

A city-block-long sign announces a Broadway show: "Cats. Now and Forever at the Winter Garden Theater."

A billboard on a commuter train promotes a lottery and shows an average-looking man drinking a beer sitting in a palatial high-ceilinged living room: "Lotto. Hey: you never know."

A red, white, and black sign featuring a tall chef's hat features the words: "Manero's Restaurant: Always Bring the Children!"

A sign depicts a sheet of lined paper taken from a child's composition notebook that announces in marking pen, "TAG SALE TODAY!"

Rule 2. Use symbols and icons.

Your customers are accustomed to interpreting symbols. The symbols for deer, school crossings, or children playing, for example, have become a uniformly understood visual sign language.

Today, the growing popularity of the Internet and Windows has increased the "visual literacy" of the average customer. A nontechnical person, for example, can sit down and begin to operate a PC using Windows by guessing at the function of icons from their design, often with amazing accuracy.

Any symbols or icons prominently featured in your advertising and printed literature should be carried over to signage. If you don't have such icons, consider creating them. A circle atop an upside-down triangle, for instance, is a clear, simple way to communicate that you sell ice cream cones. Planets orbiting the sun would be perfect for a planetarium.

Rule 3. Establish an objective.

Signs are the most direct form of visual communication available. They perform several major communication functions for your business, including:

- Directing customers to your store
- Providing information about your business
- Announcing sales and specials
- Selling and persuading
- Communicating an image, message, or impression
- Generating inquires to a toll-free 800 number
- Generating visits to your Web site

Signs cover a territory so people can find you ("Take Exit 6, 2 miles ahead, for Shoney's Restaurant"). Such signs are designed for travelers, new members of a community, and impulse shoppers who want to find you to purchase the particular goods or services you sell ("Tag Sale, 2 P.M., at 333 Essex Court"). If your business is located at a site that is not well trafficked, your sign can, in part, overcome this disability through effective communication. Signs, however, point customers to you regardless of where you are.

Because of space limitations, you should have only one major objective for each sign or billboard and stick with it. If you want drivers to know that your store is located just off turnpike exit 14B, make that your main message. Don't clutter it with extraneous material.

Rule 4. Make your signs noticeable and readable.

Your customers are moving targets. They usually read your signs while in motion. So you don't have time for a lengthy sales pitch. Signs must be quick, clear, and to the point. The Absolut vodka, Camel cigarettes, and American Airlines billboards are bold and vivid. The American Airlines billboard shows a clock that emphasizes the fact that the airline offers hourly service from LaGuardia to O'Hare Airport in Chicago.

Use short phrases to complete sentences. Boil your message down to its essence. If you sell flowers and can only fit one word on your sign, that word should be *FLOWERS*.

Use dark letters against a light background or light letters on a dark background. Contrast should be high. If the letters are too close in color to the background, they won't be readable.

The Institute of Outdoor Advertising tells advertisers: "The fewer the words, the larger the illustration, the bolder the colors, the simpler the background, and the clearer the product identification, the better the outdoor advertisement."

Rule 5. Add motion and light.

Although somewhat more costly than conventional two-dimensional signage, signs that incorporate motion or light are especially effective at grabbing attention. A good example: the Day-Glo menu boards used in restaurants on which the names of the dishes are written in bright illuminated colors against a black background.

Are you a financial services firm? Maybe a digital display built into your sign can show the interest accruing on your clients' funds which you manage for them. Do you have a convenience store that saves buyers time? How about incorporating a clock into your sign? Have a travel agency? Consider a model of a jet suspended on a wire between two islands against the backdrop of a sunny blue sky.

If you don't have the budget for this, don't fret. Often 3-D effects can be achieved using clever graphic techniques on 2-D surfaces.

Rule 6. Design signs that promote your image.

At times the person who writes the ad is also the same person who makes decisions about the graphics that will enhance the copy.

Thomas Lavey, president of Lakeland Outdoor in Manitowoc, Wisconsin, offers this advice on design: "Try to come up with a graphic or visual that tells the story. If you have to add copy, use a play on words—it will result in a more memorable message."

One antifreeze company's copy was: "You Go In Snow—Or we Pay The Tow."

If you are creating signs for a business, sign design can reinforce a certain tone: Stark, simple design and materials may suggest discount prices and no frills. Elegant and expensive sign materials may suggest luxury goods and services.

Two basic design considerations are physical elements and graphic elements.

Physical elements include size, placement, materials, and structure. The size of the sign is an important consideration. A sign that is either too big or too small will not communicate your message effectively. The biggest sign that you can afford may not necessarily be the best one for your needs. Although a sign should be appropriate for its environment—signs in upscale spas, hotels, or pharmacies, for example, have to reflect the tone of these enterprises—you may purposely design a sign meant to stand out. One Connecticut antique shop hung a sign by the road saying, "Westbrook Antique Center: You won't find anything new in here!"

Graphic elements include layout of the message, lettering, colors, symbolism, harmony, and daytime vs. nighttime lighting conditions. Legibility means the ability to read the letters or characters on the sign. Letters and characters should distinct from one another. Certain color combinations of background and letters make the characters much more legible than others. At long distances a bold, black, serif typeface will be more readable than a sans serif typeface. Dark letters against a light background will have a greater impact than light letters against a dark background.

To test your sign's legibility, drive past it and see if you can read it from a distance. Look at it both during the day and at night. A well-designed sign should be attention-getting and original while appropriate to its purpose.

Index

About the Authors

Bob Bly has been an independent copywriter since 1982. He has written hundreds of ads, direct-mail packages, brochures, sales letters, press releases, and other promotional materials for more than 100 companies in the United States and overseas. His clients have included IBM, AT&T, Agora Publishing, EBI Medical Systems, Brooklyn Union Gas, PSE&G, Corestates Financial Corporation, BOC Gases, Value Line, McGraw-Hill, Institutional Investor Journals, Medical Economics, Allied Signal, ITT Fluid Technology, Associated Air Freight, Lucent Technologies, and M&T Chemicals.

Bob Bly is the author of more than 35 books, including *The Copywriter's Handbook* (Henry Holt & Co.), *The Advertising Manager's Handbook* (Prentice Hall), *The Perfect Sales Piece* (John Wiley & Sons), and *Power-Packed Direct Mail* (Henry Holt & Co.). His articles have appeared in such publications as *Direct Marketing, Business Marketing, Computer Decisions, Chemical Engineering, Writer's Digest, Amtrak Express, New Jersey Monthly,* and *Direct.* He is a frequent speaker at direct-marketing industry events and has taught copywriting at New York University.

Prior to becoming a freelance copywriter, Bly was advertising manager for Koch Engineering and a staff copywriter for Westinghouse. A winner of the Direct Marketing Association's Gold Echo Award for Best Direct Mail Package of the Year, Bob is a member of the Business Marketing Association. He can be reached at: Bob Bly, The Center for Technical Communication, 22 E. Quackenbush Avenue, Dumont, NJ 07628, phone (201) 385-1220.

Gary Blake, Ph.D., director of The Communication Workshop, has developed writing, presentation, interpersonal, and selling skills seminars for more than 250 organizations throughout the United States,

175

Canada, and Europe. These organizations include American Airlines Decisions Technology, The American Stock Exchange, Bayer, CSX Transportation, Lever Brothers, Manitoba Telephone Systems, Oxford Health Plans, Price Waterhouse, Symbol Technologies, and United Healthcare.

Among the seminars he has designed and presented are Effective Bus-iness Writing, Technical Writing for Engineers, Technical Writing for Systems Professionals, Persuasive Writing, Grammar and Punctuation, Presentation Skills, Writing for ISO 9000, and Writing Effective Direct Mail.

Gary Blake's tenth book, *Quick Tips for Better Business Writing,* was recently published by McGraw-Hill. He holds a B.S. and M.S. in Communications from the University of Wisconsin and a doctorate from the City University of New York. His articles have appeared in publications ranging from the *New York Times Book Review* and *Family Circle,* to the *Wall Street Journal* and *Advertising Age.* Dr. Blake can be reached at: Gary Blake, The Communication Workshop, 130 Shore Road, Port Washington, NY 11050, phone (516) 767-9590.

Together, Blake and Bly have coauthored seven books, including *How to Promote Your Own Business* (New American Library), *The Elements of Business Writing* (Macmillan), and *The Elements of Technical Writing* (Macmillan).

exceptional and essential guides for every aspect of your professional life

One way or another, we all have to communicate during the course of a day. The Elements of. . . series of guides are user-friendly and packed with hands-on examples, making it easy to learn or improve our skills. Whatever your field of expertise, they're indispensable!

The Elements of Business Writing
The Essential Guide to Writing Clear, Concise Letters, Memos, Reports, Proposals, and Other Business Documents
by Gary Blake and Robert W. Bly
ISBN 0-02-008095-6 • $9.95 • paper

The Elements of Correspondence
How to Express Yourself Clearly, Persuasively, and Eloquently in Your Personal and Business Writing
by Mary A. De Vries
ISBN 0-02-531305-3 • $19.95 • cloth
ISBN 0-02-860840-2 • $9.95 • paper

The Elements of Editing
A Modern Guide for Editors and Journalists
by Arthur Plotnik
ISBN 0-02-861451-8 • $9.95 • paper

The Elements of Grammar
The Essential Guide to Refining and Improving Grammar—from the Basics of Sentence Structure to the Art of Composing Written Works
by Margaret Shertzer
ISBN 0-02-861449-6 • $9.95 • paper

The Elements of Legal Writing
A Guide to the Principles of Writing Clear, Concise, and Persuasive Legal Documents
by Martha Faulk and Irving M. Mehler
ISBN 0-02-860839-9 • $9.95 • paper

The Elements of Nonsexist Usage
A Guide to Inclusive Spoken and Written English
by Val Dumond
ISBN 0-13-368911-5 • $4.95 • paper

The Elements of Playwriting
How to Write Stageworthy Plays, Develop Your Theatre Sense, Create Theatrical Characters, Shape Plot and Dialogue, and Find the Resources to Get Your Play Produced
by Louis E. Catron
ISBN 0-02-069291-9 • $10.00 • paper

The Elements of Screenwriting
The Essential Guide to Creating Successful Film and Television Scripts—from the Initial Idea, through Plot, Character, and Dialogue Development, to the Finished Work
by Irwin R. Blacker
ISBN 0-02-861450-X • $9.95 • paper

The Elements of Speechwriting and Public Speaking
The Essential Guide to Preparing and Delivering Powerful, Eloquent, and Well-Received Speeches, Reducing Panic and Nervousness, and Enjoying all Types of Speaking Engagements
by Jeff Scott Cook
ISBN 0-02-861452-6 • $9.95 • paper

The Elements of Technical Writing
The Essential Guide to Writing Clear, Concise Proposals, Reports, Manuals, Letters, Memos, and Other Documents in Every Technical Field
by Gary Blake and Robert W. Bly
ISBN 0-02-013085-6 • $9.95 • paper

All Elements of. . . titles are available in your local bookstore

or call toll-free to order
1-800-428-5331